TAKE CHARGE OF YOUR LIFE

Robert L. Backman

Deseret Book Company
Salt Lake City, Utah

Contents

Take Charge of Your Life

Recently I talked to a man who has been successful in his life. He seems to have been in the right places at the right times, and fortune has smiled favorably on him. Someone once said to him, "You know, you really are a lucky man." He responded, "Yes, that's true, I am a lucky man, and I'd be the first to acknowledge that fact. But you know, it's a funny thing—it seems as if the harder I work, the luckier I get."

There is a lot of wisdom in his little joke. People who rely on luck to pull them through often seem to get a lot of luck, but a good part of it is either bad or mediocre. Those who are prepared to take advantage of an opportunity when it drops on them are those who seem to be the "lucky" ones.

This appears to be true in every field of endeavor. Many of our greatest scientific and technical discoveries, for example, have been made apparently by accident. But the accidents have usually happened to those who have been working hard on the problem. When Charles Goodyear's experimental concoction bubbled over on the stove, he accidently discovered the answer to his quest on how to vulcanize rubber.

The well-known story of Sir Isaac Newton sitting under a tree when an apple fell on his head illustrates the same point. Innumerable people have had apples and other objects fall on their heads in the course of mankind's history. Most of us just rub the sore spot and complain. But for Newton, that lucky bounce off his cranium stirred up the gray matter inside, and eventually he produced a system of physics that brought order for a time to man's understanding of the entire cosmos. A lucky bounce? Well, yes, but when a woman reportedly asked Sir Isaac Newton how he discovered the law of gravity, he replied, "By thinking about it all the time."

Now, we won't all restructure the universe in the minds of men, but we all have significant and important things that we can accomplish in our lives if we have the proper approach and attitude regarding the things that happen to us. Perhaps that is the key phrase. Many people go through their lives letting things *happen to them,* but a few go through their lives *happening to things.* They are the shakers, the movers, the directors, the programmers not only of their own lives, but also of the lives of those with whom they come in contact. And these motivators are not all rich, famous, and historic.

One of the most effective people I know is a high school student. She seems never to suffer from the boredom and frustration, the indecision and lack of direction that afflict so many young people. She is always active, always has friends, always has something going, always has a sparkle in her eye.

One day I asked her how she achieved this kind of exciting life. She acknowledged modestly that she had good friends and a good family and was fortunate in a number of other ways. But as we talked, I began to see a side of her that she was a little modest and reluctant to reveal. She showed me the schedule she makes up at the beginning of every week. On her little calendar are all the obligations she has committed herself to: homework, civic volunteer duties, and church activities as well as the household jobs that are a trial in the life of every teenager. In addition, she had a file of resource material that she used to make other plans. She clipped articles in the newspaper on upcoming activities in her community. She kept notes on friends she would like to do things with. She had a calendar of upcoming movies she would like to see and a schedule of the following week's TV programs.

From these resources, my friend made up a schedule of activities for each day, things she had to do and things she wanted to do. Her schedule would change as unpredicted events arose, but it gave her a basis to work from. The list was made in order of importance, so if she didn't get everything on her list done in a day, at least she knew she would be working on the most important one she had yet to do.

She also kept a few notes in the back of her book about things she would someday like to do. Some of them were pipe dreams; some were practical, long-range goals. But they were all giving direction to her life. She would not arrive somewhere someday and be surprised. Life would not just happen to her. She would happen to it.

I strongly believe this is one of the secrets to living life to its fullest. This is a great part of the message that Jesus came to deliver to us. He said, "I am come that they might have life, and that they might have it more abundantly" (John 10:10), and "Ye shall know the truth, and the truth shall make you free" (John 8:32).

This is one of those great truths that Jesus spoke of that will make us free and give us the more abundant life.

The truth is that we are free to act and not merely be acted upon, free to take our lives in hand. No matter how exalted or humble our station, how great or limited our opportunities may appear to be, or how "lucky" or "unlucky" may be our lot in life, we need not be dictated to by circumstance. So let us not drift with the stream or enslave ourselves to habits that bind us down. Let us not deceive ourselves that there is some sort of giant roulette wheel in the universe that spins out success and happiness to some and failure and misery to others. The secret, the variable, the deciding factor is not out there in some cosmic game of chance, but here in our hearts. And if we are not yet all we would like to be, let us remember the words of Shakespeare, "The fault . . . is not in our stars, / But in ourselves." (*Julius Caesar*, I, ii, 139-40.)

If the fault is in ourselves that we are not all we would like to be, the answer is also there. By taking responsibility for our lives, exercising trust and faith in the Lord, and applying our best efforts in a systematic plan, we can achieve the happiness we seek.

To Thine Own Self Be True

Tonight if it is a moonless night, there is a very good chance that a darkened airplane will swoop low over the Florida Everglades. A deadly bag of drugs will be dropped to smugglers waiting below in the swamps. They will speed away into the darkness to peddle their derangement and death on the streets of America. And a law enforcement officer who could have arrested the smugglers and confiscated the drugs will do nothing, because he has been paid to look the other way.

This officer is one of a very small minority in the ranks of the thousands of dedicated lawmen who protect us. Far more common are brave men like Fred McKnight, narcotics agent for the Los Angeles Police Department. He recently put his life and skill on the line and broke up an international drug ring that had ruined the lives of untold victims.

It is the Fred McKnights that hold this world together, but unfortunately there are also those among us who cave in to temptation, like the first officer mentioned. His decision is one we must all make, so let's look a little closer at him.

Radio newsman Paul Harvey commented recently that we should understand the great temptations associated with the officer's job and the jobs of others like him. Just by turning his head, he could make in one night as much as he would in his entire career of difficult and dangerous police work. We need to understand the officer's position, the commentator said.

Well, I have no argument that our law enforcement people are underappreciated and overworked in these days of rising crime rates. I also agree that we are all human and subject to human failures and weaknesses. But none of this can change the rock-ribbed, everlasting, unchangeable, irrefutable, immutable truth that a person sets his own price for himself; that he's worth just about what he chooses to be worth.

So we may ask, how much is *our* integrity worth? Suppose the offer were not just a lifetime's wages, but real estate totaling 57.2 million square miles, with all the rich minerals of the sea, the gross national products of every nation, and the financial holdings of every individual on earth—in short, all the riches of the world—thrown in. Does this present a better bargain?

Jesus said, "For what is a man advantaged, if he gain the whole world, and lose himself, or be cast away!" (Luke 9:25.)

To sell our integrity is to sell life itself, according to the poet John Greenleaf Whittier. He wrote, "When faith is lost, when honor dies, /The man is dead!" ("Ichabod," st. 8.)

It is not easy to stand up for what you believe. It never has been, and it is not by accident that the world is set up this way. Otherwise how could you tell if you had integrity or not?

Walter Lippmann wrote back in 1929 that a person has honor "if he holds himself to an ideal of conduct though it is inconvenient, unprofitable, or dangerous to do so." (*A Preface to Morals*, New York: Time Inc., p. 209.)

Doing the right thing when it is also the easy thing or the

profitable thing is not a sign of integrity. That's like high-jumping without a crossbar. Anybody can do it. President David O. McKay once said that the greatest battles of life are fought within the silent chambers of the human heart, and he was right. Those are the real battles of life or death.

The victories and defeats of those inward battles show themselves in our outward actions. The story is told of a man who built houses for a living. Toward the end of his long career he was contacted by a prominent citizen who engaged him to build a beautiful home. The man was well-to-do, and he told the builder to spare no expense, but to make it the finest home he could construct.

The builder began with great dreams and good plans. But as he proceeded with the house, he found himself in some financial difficulty. And so he began to cut the quality of the home—nothing you could see on the outside, but deep inside in the plumbing and the wiring, the internal supports and insulation, he used second-rate materials and quick and shoddy workmanship. He knew the home would look as he had designed it on the outside, though in a few years it would begin to show the lack of workmanship within. Nevertheless, given the pressures he was under, he felt justified in cutting corners. His conscience pricked him a bit, but he put it down, telling himself that the man for whom he was building the home was surely wealthy enough to have it repaired or even replaced if necessary.

Finally the day came when the builder presented the new and apparently beautiful home to its new owner—and the builder received the shock of his life. The wealthy customer said, "I have watched you for many years and admired the things you have built. At this, the close of your career, I thought, 'What fitting gesture could I make of my admiration for you?' It came to me that the best testament of a man's life is the work he has done. And so I am presenting to you the keys and the deed to this beautiful home. It will stand as a memorial to the kind of work that you have done."

And thus it did.

This may or may not be a true story, but the point behind it is as true as every thought we think and every act we perform. Each of us is building our own dwelling place in the course of our life. The view from the street might indicate that some have had the materials to build palaces while others have been limited to constructing a cottage. But the size and the elegance of the structure are not important. The internal integrity is. Each of us will be given the keys and the deed to our stately or shabby structures and invited to live there knowing full well whether or not the walls are sound, the roof tight, the foundation firm.

Someone has said that after about age forty, each of us pretty much deserves the face he is wearing. He designed it from the inside. That's part of what makes life so exciting. We can be anything we want to be, but we must build solidly on a foundation of honor and integrity.

In *Hamlet*, Shakespeare's famous play, a character named Polonius speaks some words of wisdom that have come down through the centuries. He said, "This above all: to thine own self be true, /And it must follow, as the night the day, / Thou canst not then be false to any man." (*Hamlet*, I, iii, 78-80.)

Become a Self-Starter

Back in 1912, the Cadillac motorcar company invented a gadget that became a great boon to drivers, particularly to ladies and to people stalled on railroad tracks. It was a little motor nestled down in the innards of the engine. It was not much to look at, but marvelous to experience, because it turned the automobile into a self-starter. No more fumbling to get the crank out from under the front seat and stick it into the business end of your buggy. No more calisthenics trying to get the temperamental thing to turn over. No more broken thumbs when the engine backfired, and no more leaping out of the car's path and into the front seat to keep from being run over or run away from. The self-starter was a marvelous page in the history of science's service to man.

That small motor has a parallel in our own lives. It doesn't take a lot of power to get started, but it can make all the difference in the world. People who are self-starting get a real jump on those that have to be cranked, and in the long run, that can spell victory or defeat in the journey of life.

Nicholas Murray Butler, former chancellor of Columbia University, once said that there are three kinds of people: those who make things happen, those who watch things happen, and those who have no idea of what is happening.

9

People who direct the course of the world as well as their own lives are in the first category, those who make things happen.

At first it may seem an awesome burden to take upon yourself the responsibility of your own life, along with the weight of the morning mattress clinging to your back. But as with any other accomplishment or ability, you can break down the self-starting skills into bite-sized bits that make the job more digestable.

Or to change the metaphor, here is a simple road map to help you get to your destination. *The first step* is to try to gain a victory every day. You needn't change the course of the world's direction; even a small but satisfying victory can give you peaceful rest at the end of the day. But something needs to go right for you sometime between each rising of the sun. The size of the victory is not important, but the consistency is.

I remember when my daughter came to me in her first self-tied shoes. Alexander the Great could not have worn a wider smile of accomplishment when he conquered the world than did my little girl when she gained the victory over those two maverick shoelaces.

The second step to the success of self-starters is to have a plan, a procedure worked out in advance, one you know works. This will build your confidence. Again, if at first it is more modest than miraculous, that's all right. The important thing is that it works, that it gives you a feeling of success, for success builds confidence. We all work from habit patterns, so choose the habits and procedures that have brought you success in the past, and drop into them when you find yourself getting bogged down.

The third step is to set deadlines for your accomplishments. Few of us actually enjoy being pressed by deadlines, but without them, the world tends to move on without us. The things we plan to do "sometime" rarely get done, because sometime is no time. One of Murphy's well-known laws is that work expands to fill the time allotted to it. So set aside the time you feel is necessary and then set a deadline at that point.

Frank Morrison, a famous novelist, tells about basking on the beach in the Caribbean, sure the sun and sand would stir his creativity, but just the opposite happened. His sun-basking brain couldn't seem to string a single subject and predicate together. It only took one telegram from his banker back home, telling him that at the end of the month he would be broke, and suddenly the creative juices fairly gushed as he rushed to beat the deadline.

The fourth step in the self-starting process is to keep in mind your rewards, the fruits of your present toil. Those re-wards may be monetary if that is the business you're work-ing on, or they may be more lasting rewards, such as good friends, peace of mind, a healthy body. In the middle of an exercise program, you need to plant firmly in your mind a picture of that splendid physical specimen you plan to be. Only then can you keep the jogging steps, the swimming strokes, the pushups, or the bicycle pedals moving.

This four-step program will help you become a self-starter or improve on your present abilities. But the next question is, how do we self-start a self-starting program? Wise old King Solomon in the Bible said, "With all thy getting, get understanding." (Proverbs 4:7.) Someone para-phrased Solomon and said, "With all thy getting, get going." There is no better bit of advice. The best plan ever concocted did not accomplish anything sitting on a shelf. Goethe, a man of genius in several fields, said, "Are you in earnest? Seize this very minute; what you can do, or dream you can, begin it! Boldness has genius, power and magic in it. Only engage, and then the mind grows heated; begin, and the task is half completed."

Beginning is a big secret to success in this world. No

matter how awesome the undertaking, it will have a beginning. As the Chinese proverb says, "A journey of a thousand miles begins with one step."

Certainly you need to analyze the situation, plot your course as best you can, and weigh the outcomes, but then the time comes for beginning. Undoubtedly you will make some mistakes. The only people who don't make mistakes are people who do nothing, and that is the biggest mistake of all. But so long as you are alive and moving, those errors can be corrected. You can change course, modify plans, and reset your directions.

The story is told of a young man who made many mistakes. He persecuted, harassed, and intimidated people. He even held the coats of a mob who committed murder. He was sadly misled and misdirected, but he was a dynamic, driving personality. When he literally saw the light, he changed his life and put his energy into the cause to which he was converted. And no man did more to spread the gospel of Jesus Christ in that day than did this dedicated missionary, Paul.

On the other hand, the Bible speaks of the lazy and lukewarm in these words: "Thou art neither cold nor hot: I would thou wert cold or hot. So then because thou art lukewarm, and neither cold nor hot, I will spue thee out of my mouth." (Revelations 3:15.)

Why be lukewarm when, with a little more fire, you could be a force for good, a self-starter?

How Will You Get from Here to There?

Come and walk with me along the dock at one of the world's greatest natural harbors, the bay of San Francisco. Here we will see all kinds of ships: gigantic freighters, beautiful ocean liners, oil tankers, and ore carriers, big ships of most every size and shape and flying the flags of many nations.

If we were privileged to go up onto the bridge of each of these ships and talk with their captains, we would likewise find them to be different one from another. Some would be tall, some short, some fair, and some dark. They, like their ships, would be many and varied, but there is one way in which I can guarantee you they would be exactly alike. As each of them sets out to sea, if we were to ask them where they are bound, they would be able to tell us. Not a single solitary sailor among them would say, "Well, I think I'll just take this big ship and this precious cargo out into the ocean and sort of see what develops. I may find some direction out there that strikes my fancy, or maybe I'll just tag along with the crowd, if that looks like fun." I can guarantee you that if we did find a captain who talked like that, he wouldn't be captain very long.

Now let's take a quick hop across the country to Cape

Canaveral, Florida, and stand with the scientists and the technicians and their banks of TV monitors, computers, and other twentieth-century technical wizardry. We are waiting for the final countdown of an interplanetary rocket.

This time we'll assume that the officials in charge know where the rocket is bound. But suppose we asked them and they gave us an answer like this: "See that one planet up there? It's about, oh, two inches to the left of that real bright star; yeah, well, we figured we'd kind of like to send it up there."

And we would say, "How interesting. How do you plan to get there?"

He might say, "Get there? Why, you can see it from here. So we're just going to point the rocket at it, and let her rip. Ten, nine, eight, seven, six . . ."

We'll do a merciful fade out on that scene. In this case, the people sort of know where they would like to go, but they really haven't worked out the steps to take them there.

These two stories are fictitious, of course. We all know that rockets and ships are much too valuable to be launched this way. But something far more valuable gets launched every day in an even more haphazard manner. That something valuable is people. People who every day set out on life's voyage either with no conception of where they want to go or with vague generalizations of places like happiness, or comfort, or security. The odds that they will drift into the right port or bump into the right star are just about as unfavorable as setting adrift in an open ocean or blasting off into an untracked sky.

I talked awhile back to a young man in high school. He has three older brothers who are all remarkably successful in their fields. I wondered what this family had going for it, so I struck up a conversation. After a couple of pleasantries, I said, "Evan, what are your plans?"

The question was a little ambiguous, and I meant it to

be so. A lot of us might have said, "I don't know," or "Right after work I plan to go home, have supper, watch a little TV, maybe catch a movie . . ." A few of us who really like to think ahead might have said, "Well, if the weather holds, I plan to go skiing this Saturday."

But this young man whipped out an answer that came so fast and naturally that it was more like a reflex action off his spinal cord than a ponderous decision in his brain. He said, "I'm planning to take a few more biology classes in high school and then get into premed at college. I can get in two semesters before my mission, and then afterwards the ROTC has a program that will help me through school. After I've filled my obligation to them, I plan to go into private practice."

Do you think that young man will be successful? Firmly imbedded in his mind are the steps it will take to get him where he wants to be, and he has committed the resources in time and energy to accomplish those steps. I'll book passage on his ship any time.

Dr. Maxwell Maltz wrote a book several years ago titled *Psycho-Cybernetics*, in which he compared the brain to the functions of an advanced computer. The most dramatic examples of these smart computers are the guidance systems in space rockets. Built into their program is a feedback function that tells them whether or not they are traveling the right course through space. If not, they will automatically adjust and get back on course.

Dr. Maltz says that the human subconscious functions in somewhat the same way. It is "telelogical" in nature. That is, it is concerned with endings, destinations, and goals. Dr. Maltz contends that if a person can just tell the subconscious in strong and explicit terms where he wants to go, it will find a way for him to get there. (*Psycho-Cybernetics*, New York: Fireside Books, 1960, pp. 16-22.)

The key is to decide what destination you want, set it

firmly in your mind, and then feed that information into your guidance system as clearly and as distinctly and as often as it takes to keep you on target.

Goal setting is not easy; that is why so little of it is done. But it is the only way to get where you really want to go. What better time than now to lay out your goals in front of you, write them down, analyze them carefully, picture them in your mind, and constantly keep them before you.

The book of Proverbs in the Old Testament says that "where there is no vision, the people perish." (Proverbs 29:18.) The same is true of individuals, so catch a vision of what you can become, then select your goals and set out to reach them.

Look to the Lord for Help

In the Old Testament, the story is told of a national heartache, an entire people who dreamed a dream and then missed it.

You may recall that when the Children of Israel fled from Egypt, their hope was to hurry back to the promised land, that country given to their father Abraham so long ago by the Lord. The promised land. How the thought of it must have echoed in the talk of this people, comforted the weary days of slavery, sparkled like a gem before them in the drabness of existence. Perhaps their children or their children's children would live to see it. Rumors of a deliverer had been whispered among them for generations, and when the Lord finally sent Moses, and Israel marched forth into the desert toward Canaan, their land, what a day it must have been.

A few months later the Children of Israel were camped before the entrance to the land. The Lord told Moses to send twelve men to search out the country and bring back word about living conditions there. Were the people there strong or weak, few or many? Did they live in tents or strongholds? Was the land fat or lean?

After spending forty days on their mission, the twelve men returned. They brought back figs, pomegranates, and a stock of grapes so large it had to be carried on a pole between two men. This was a land of milk and honey, and Joshua and Caleb, two of the explorers, were eager to go up and possess it, believing Israel was well able to overcome it. But the other men were not so eager. The land would eat its inhabitants, they said. The people who dwelt there were such giants that the scouts had crawled before them like grasshoppers. They described the cities as walled fortresses, concluding "We be not able to go up against the people."

At the men's fierce tales, the congregation of Israel began to moan and wail. "Would God that we had died in the land of Egypt! . . . Wherefore hath the Lord brought us unto this land, to fall by the sword, that our wives and our children should be a prey?"

Caleb and Joshua tried to stop the self-pity and fear of the Israelites and plead with them to listen. "If the Lord delight in us, then he will bring us into this land, and give it us; a land which floweth with milk and honey. Only rebel not ye against the Lord, neither fear ye the people of the land; for . . . the Lord is with us; fear them not."

These words fell on deaf ears. The people were too paralyzed with anxiety to hear. In their minds, the walled cities and the strong giants of Canaan were more powerful than the Lord himself. This was a people who had been led by the Lord out of the most powerful empire in the world. "They had been personal witnesses to plagues that afflicted the Egyptians but left Israel untouched. They had with their own hands smeared blood on the doorways of their homes and then heard the cries of the Egyptians as their firstborn fell. They had walked between towering walls of water that divided at the command of Moses, then watched as those walls collapsed on the armies of the pharaoh. They ate bread that miraculously appeared each morning, drank water gushing from a rock, felt Sinai quake, and saw it glow with fire. What people in all of history had greater witness that God was with them and would use His unsurpassable power in their behalf?" *(Old Testament Manual, Genesis— 2 Samuel,* The Church of Jesus Christ of Latter-day Saints, p. 205.)

But incredibly, it was not enough. Even with the Lord to help them, the Israelites would not go up into Canaan, and they were therefore cursed to wander in the desert forty more years until the whole fainthearted generation except Joshua and Caleb had died. They had come within miles of the country they had waited generations to inhabit, but they would never walk upon its roads. (See Numbers 13, 14.)

Now this is a tragedy as ancient as Israel, but with principles as enduring as the earth itself. It was true then, and continues to be so, that any prize worth owning will be guarded by fierce giants. In fact, it is usually true that the best prizes are guarded by the fiercest giants. These giants may take many forms—obstacles to hurdle, weaknesses to trample, hard labor to perform—but you can be sure that any goal worth its salt will take mighty struggling to reach. Along the way there may be sacrifice, there may be pain, there may be hours when you seriously contemplate giving up your dream. Giving up is so much easier—or so it seems. Yet the path of least resistance is the path to nowhere. Those who follow it don't master their bad habits, don't achieve their dreams—don't, it seems, enter the promised land. They are left to a lifetime of wandering, and their prizes are awarded to someone else.

The picture of the Children of Israel trembling before the land for which they had waited for generations may be a reflection of all mankind cowering before their aspirations when they see how rough the road is between here and there.

It was true then, and continues to be so, that the Lord and one man—any man—are a majority. Mortals are too impressed by what seems immediate, the clanking of armies, the walls around cities, the push and pull of their everyday world. The Israelites did not believe the Lord could help them conquer the people who lived in Canaan, not just because they were spineless and forgetful of what He had already done for them, but because they were hungry and tired and overwhelmed with the sheer immediacy of what lay before them. It takes faith to see beyond the urgencies of the very minute, faith to follow what is not immediately tangible. Like many of us, the Israelites did not have such faith, and so they spent the rest of their lives eating dust when they could have been eating milk and honey.

But Caleb and Joshua, the only two of the thousands who left Egypt, did finally pitch their tents in Canaan, because of the courage and belief that filled them. They held on to their great work and did not retreat from the battle, no matter how terrible it became. When they were completing the conquest of Canaan forty-five years after that initial exploration, Caleb said to Joshua, "Forty years old was I when Moses the servant of the Lord sent me . . . to espy out the land; and I brought him word again as it was in mine heart. Nevertheless my brethren that went up with me made the heart of the people melt; but I wholly followed the Lord my God. . . .

"And now, behold, the Lord hath kept me alive, as he said, these forty and five years. . . . And yet I am as strong this day as I was in the day that Moses sent me; as my strength was then, even so is my strength now, . . . both to go out, and come in."

From these words it is easy to see that Caleb was still a believer in himself, in his purpose, and in the Lord. And Caleb concluded his declaration by looking around the land still inhabited by the giants, seeing that they needed yet to be overcome, and taking the challenge. "Give me this mountain," he said to Joshua. "If . . . the Lord will be with me, then I shall be able to drive them out." (Joshua 14:7-8, 10-12.)

Ahead of you are enormous challenges, work to be done, and purposes to be accomplished; and you can be sure that as you set out to meet them, you will meet obstacles. Sometimes you will want to ask of life, "Give me a small hill." But you must keep Caleb's attitude. Give me this mountain. Give me this challenge. Give me this great mission. What must be done can be done. A promised land or promised blessing can be yours if you will take your challenges and look to the Lord to help you meet them.

Six Basic Rules
of Success

The other day I was in a meeting when a man two rows ahead of me slumped down in his chair. It was obvious he was in trouble. The people nearby stretched him out on the floor, and someone went for a doctor. The doctor hurried in, surveyed the scene, loosened the man's tie and shirt collar, gave him a couple of strong thumps on the chest, and started mouth-to-mouth resuscitation. In a matter of moments the man was breathing normally.

If that doctor had had to get his emergency manual and start to read the instructions, it would have been all over for the man on the floor. But the doctor was prepared, so he was successful.

Life is like that. We talk about luck and the fortunes of fate and the coincidences by which one person succeeds and another fails. True, we don't know all the factors that go into making one person a success and another a failure. But I think we are mistaken if we assume that everything is left to chance.

There are some definite principles that lead to success. A friend of mine who is a college president, Rodney H. Brady, gives to all the athletes who come to his school a little card with six rules that lead to success. And being prepared is one of them.

A second rule for success is to find that extra ounce of effort when you don't have any more. Years ago I sat in the stadium of a college and watched a mile race. A young man from the University of Wyoming was picked to finish first, and as the race progressed, it was obvious why. He had a beautiful, smooth stride. Nobody could touch him. But I didn't find until the last lap of the race what else he had. Something had gone wrong that day: either he was not feeling well, or the altitude or the temperature got to him, or he had misjudged the race. At the end of three and a half of the four laps, he was exhausted. It seemed obvious that he could not finish.

The other runners were considerably behind him, but they saw immediately that he was in trouble. This gave them encouragement to quicken their pace, and they began to close the gap rapidly. The leader struggled and floundered as his coordination seemed to come unglued. The smooth grace was replaced by a stumbling stagger. He couldn't go another ten yards.

But he did. Then another ten, then another twenty. The other runners were gaining on him fast, but he would not quit. He staggered and struggled across the finish line a fraction of a foot in front of the others, then collapsed on the track.

I saw that day not only the legs and lungs of a fine runner, but also the heart of a champion who wouldn't quit. When you've given it everything you've got, then you need to reach way down deep and give a little bit more.

A third rule of success that I believe is true is that successful people help the team rather than just an individual succeed. World War II produced some brave men and heroic deeds. Perhaps the best known of all these brave men holds no medals, however. He once did. He was once the most decorated soldier in the United States military. But he gave his medals all back, saying he couldn't keep them. Why? "Because," he replied, "everything I did was the work of a team. Everybody was doing his part."

Audie Murphy had learned a principle that we might all remember, that true success comes when the team wins. None of us can do very much alone.

The fourth and fifth rules of success are to follow the leader and to set clear goals. I have hiked a lot of miles with scout troups. We have overcome mountains, blisters, burned pancakes, homesickness—all the challenges that come with being twelve years old in the great outdoors. And I guess I've learned one thing above all else: When we followed our leader and could see where we were going, we could make it. The goal might have been a mountain peak off on the horizon or a refreshing spring just around the bend. Whatever it was, it was vitally important that we knew what our goal was and how we planned to get there.

The successful people I know have carried that principle with them like a compass. At any time in their life, if you ask them where they are going and how they plan to get there, they can tell you. Oh, they might not take the exact route they laid out, but they wouldn't just wander around and hope to arrive at their destination. Having a goal, having a plan to reach it, and having the will power to follow those plans—those are great keys to success.

That brings me to the sixth rule of success. Basic to all the others is the determination to grit your teeth and hang in there when the going gets tough—and it will. But as the saying goes, when the going gets tough, the tough get going. And it doesn't matter how many times we go down. What matters is how many times we get back up, how much determination we show.

Dr. Brady's little cards remind his athletes that in both athletics and life, these six things bring success: (1)

Thorough training and preparation. (2) Finding that extra ounce of effort when you don't have any more. (3) Making the team rather than just an individual succeed. (4) Following the leader, the direction of the coach. (5) Setting clear goals and laying out plans to reach those goals, and having the will power to follow those plans. (6) Having the determination to carry through with the other five.

So set worthy goals in your life, follow this procedure, and I can guarantee you that you will succeed.

Develop Self-Discipline

In this world there are no more magnificent horses than the fabled Arabians. Selectively bred for three centuries, they have developed the intelligent eyes, well-formed head, sensitive ears, flowing mane and tail, and beautiful conformation that mark their aristocratic lineage. But more than that, they have stamina and courage that have made them champions, particularly in the demanding desert country from which they take their name.

Yet even among this race of royalty, some stand above the rest. To determine which these are, the trainers take the colts and teach them to drink only when the trainer sounds a whistle. Once the horses have been thoroughly taught this principle of obedience, they are placed in a corral in the sun until they are more thirsty than they have ever been in their young lives. Then water is brought and placed outside the corral beyond their reach. But again they must wait. Finally the bar is dropped and the thirsty colts bolt out of the corral for the water. Most of them immediately stick their noses into the trough and drink with reckless abandon. But a few stand poised with their young proud heads erect and will not give in to the terrible craving within them until they hear the whistle. Then they drink.

The other horses are led away to lead normal lives, but the ones that possess the necessary self-discipline are reserved for special training as champions. As it is with these splendid horses, so it is with us. The mark of the champion is not on the outside; it is deep within the soul where self-control resides.

Bill Bradley was an all-American and all-pro basketball star. He was also a Rhodes Scholar and is a United States senator. The fans spoke of his great eye and his soft touch. Their assumption was that these were gifts he was born with. Bradley scoffs at this idea. "Soft touch?" he said. "Great eye? The secret is in shooting from one spot until you can hit twenty-five baskets consistently. The secret of scholarship is never going to bed until your assignments are finished. And the secret of success in life is self-discipline, the discipline that makes you get up on Sunday morning and go to church instead of sacking in." Bill Bradley learned what all who truly succeed have learned: that you have to pay the price.

Parry O'Brien was the first man to put the shot more than sixty feet. He threw it every night, often as many as a hundred practice heaves. "I didn't quit until my hands were bleeding," he said.

Don Schollander swam his way to three Olympic gold medals. Natural abilities? Yes, but also five hours a day every day for eight of his eighteen years. What did he develop? Skills, of course; stamina, yes; but more important than these, self-discipline to give it everything he had, and then find an extra ounce of energy to make his best a little better. "The greatest sensation in swimming is the pain you have to swim through," he said. "But the real thrill is winning—and winning big."

Wade Bell ran the half mile in the Olympics. He said, "Track is a proving ground. It's a place where my mind can make my body do something it doesn't want to do; where I

can say I did ten 440's today in sixty seconds each, and that
the last four were so hard I thought my legs would drop off,
but my mind kept me going."

Self-control is not just for youth and the athletic field.
Pablo Casals was probably the greatest cellist the world has
known. As a performer, composer, and director, he was in a
class by himself. On the day when Casals observed his
ninety-fourth birthday, reporters gathered to his home. They
probably expected to find this man who was so full of years,
accolades, and honors taking a well-earned rest. But they
found him in his studio practicing scales, the same scales
every beginning student plays, the same scales he had prac-
ticed for most of a century. Why? This master musician said
it was because it developed his discipline and led him closer
to perfection.

These are sobering examples for us who live in this day
of opportunity such as humankind has never before seen.
Never have so many had such a chance to become their best,
and particularly in America, a land of freedom and bounty.
Yet unfortunately, future historians may look back on us and
shake their heads in dismay at how much we let slip through
our fingers because of apathy. No generation of man must
acknowledge so much lost genius, so much wasted potential
as ours. For every life of dedication, we see many lives of dis-
sipation. In this century we have seen whole generations de-
clare themselves lost or "beat" or alienated. We have
watched the dropouts and the copouts. And it is not just our
youth. We have seen great segments of our society settle for a
handout, proclaiming their rights and disclaiming their responsibilities.

Among free people, self-discipline is not an option, it is
a duty. President John F. Kennedy said, "If the self-discipline
of the free cannot match the iron discipline of the mailed fist,
in economic, scientific, and all other kinds of struggles as

well as the military, then the peril of freedom will continue to rise."

Yes, we have an obligation to develop self-discipline. But we ought not be burdened, but buoyed up by this, for the promising side of this proposition is that each of us has marvelous potential just waiting to be developed through discipline. The first definition of the word is "a branch of knowledge or learning." It is we who have given the term a negative connotation.

There is nothing more stimulating than finding some little or large talent hidden within us and then working to bring it to flower. And be assured, you do have such gifts. We all do.

As Jesus indicated in his parable of the talents, some of us are given more than others. But to each of those in the parable who developed their gifts through self-discipline, the commendation from the Lord was exactly the same. And it will be the same for us if we do likewise. The Lord said, "Well done, thou good and faithful servant." (Matthew 25:21.)

Discover Who You Ought to Be

For New Year celebrations in Japan, it is the custom to eat mochi, a sticky rice cake made from pounding freshly boiled rice. Eating the confection is believed to bring good luck. But one year during the celebration, seven elderly people choked to death on the mochi. Apparently it wasn't so lucky for them.

We know we can't eat anything for luck. But many of us forget that it's what comes out of us, not what goes in, that brings us luck. Robert Louis Stevenson summed it up this way: "Worthwhile folks don't just happen. You aren't born worthwhile. You are born with the possibilities of becoming worthwhile. Your job is to discover and develop the man or woman you ought to be."

Do you think that Thomas Alva Edison, for example, just knew at birth that he was the famous Thomas Alva Edison, inventor of the light globe, someone designed to change the course of human history? Did he carry that information around with him so that it charged his days with more purpose, gave him strength for his failures? No, of course not. Being Thomas A. Edison was as obscure as being John Doe—until Thomas A. Edison did something about it. He had no guarantee that his life would be worthwhile. He made it that way.

Do you think Albert Einstein knew as a youth, when he was busy failing junior high math, that his very name would be synonymous with genius? Was he buoyed up by the fact that he, after all, was the famous and extraordinarily worthwhile Albert Einstein? No. He was born like the rest of us with a set of unrealized possibilities, his life in his own hand to design.

And what about Abraham Lincoln? Did he look in the mirror at his awkward, gangly reflection and know that he would be a man whose touch would lift millions, bind a nation bleeding and wounded? Again, no. Abraham Lincoln was no more worthwhile than any other child born into the world until he worked and made himself that way. Lincoln's own words on that point are telling. He said, "I will study and get ready, and perhaps my chance will come."

More of us ought to study and get ready. We ought to really understand that our job is to pattern our lives along the line that will unlock our best possibilities. No one can hand us self-confidence or faith in ourselves. No one can hand us knowledge or highly developed skills. They are not free gifts. They are ours to attain by hard work, and it's a lifetime task.

Now you might object, and rightfully so, that you'd have a better chance of doing well at this job if life didn't offer you so many obstacles. You're building your house of dreams, and a storm comes to collapse it. You display your best talents and are outshown. You stand ready to thrust your hand into the work of life and shrink back in fear. Obstacles. Life offers dozens of them.

Henry Ford had this to say about obstacles: "One of the great discoveries a man makes, one of his great surprises, is to find he can do what he was afraid he couldn't do. Most of the barriers we beat against are in ourselves—we put them there and we can take them down."

Let's look at just three of those self-imposed barriers.

We all have others of our own design, but most of us share at least these three.

The first barrier is that we are overcome in our quest for excellence by the trivia in our lives, the little distractions. We have great plans, but the mechanics of living take up so much time. We mean to be compassionate and kind to our neighbors, and that's just when we get a flat tire, a bill needs to be paid. We are about to give birth to a great thought, and suddenly our stomach rumbles, reminding us we're hungry. Think how many would-be writers there are with the great American novel unhatched in their hearts. "I'll do it when I get time—I'm just so busy" is the cry. That's right, we're all busy. But the big question is, what are we busy with? Television shows that we can't remember tomorrow. The mechanics of living that expand to take up the time we are willing to give them. Too often the trivialities of life daunt our dreams because we are unwilling to take time from them to concentrate our efforts. Life goes on without us while we're busy doing other things. Small distractions can destroy our living up to our possibilities.

The second barrier we erect that keeps us from our dreams is the mistaken idea that tomorrow will be better. Tomorrow it will be easier to be who we were meant to be. Tomorrow we'll have more time. Tomorrow seems to stretch a million minutes long, with plenty of time for stretching. Then tomorrow comes, and we're as cramped as we were yesterday. In fact, tomorrow has the uncanny way of feeling just like today when it gets here. If we wait until tomorrow to show our worth, if we wait to be more compassionate, more studious, more righteous, more daring, we have a long wait. Tomorrow just never comes. Waiting is a bar to our fulfilling our potential.

A third barrier to our development is that somewhere along the way, most of us lose faith in ourselves. Oh, we may not be able to pick out the precise day or incident, but we learn to somehow think of ourselves as less competent than we'd hoped. Every criticism, every mistake is bored into our consciousness, and even though we appear self-assured to the world, we carry our vulnerabilities. We cannot help but notice that others do better at some things than we do. We memorize our physical imperfections, our wrinkles. And finally we think that maybe our dream was too high for us. We learn to be what they call "realistic," and so we scale down our hopes. That's nonsense.

Probably not one of us has even begun to scratch the surface of his potential. So what if you don't do something as well as someone else. Will Rogers pointed out that every man is ignorant in one thing or another. So what if you do have imperfections, or there are times when you have failed. If you did not have these problems, you would be all alone among us here. You must not lose faith in yourself and in your possibilities. You must not simply give up and become content with mediocrity. You were meant for more than that. You were meant to do more than merely beat against your barriers, because you have probably erected all of them yourself.

Success and happiness will not come to you if you just sit back and wait for them to arrive. Excellence is never an accident. It is always a matter of a human being with wide-open eyes recognizing that this life is the time for him to grow. Opportunities fly around you every day as they do every human being on this earth. But they only belong to those with the vision to see them.

Make the Impossible Possible

Have you ever wondered why we always call past years "the good old days"? Yesterday the world seemed ripe with possibilities. To our thinking it seemed fuller, more golden, a place where a person could really make his mark. The airplane was yet to be discovered, the light bulb yet to be screwed into place. The horseless carriage could make a Henry Ford famous. Corporations were yet to be built by men and women with dreams. Frontiers were still to be conquered. Those were the days, we think, when a person could really make something of himself. And many did.

There was, for example, a little boy by the name of Heinz, living in Pennsylvania, who in 1856 grew some horseradish in a corner of his mother's garden. When it was ready, he bottled it, borrowed a wheelbarrow, and took the horseradish around to sell to the local grocers. That was the first of what became Heinz 57 Varieties.

Or what about the salesman who in 1890 watched his wife making calf's foot jelly and decided that a lot of time could be saved by powdering the gelatin. He put his idea into operation and hired salesmen to demonstrate in homes how easy it was to dissolve in water. His wife worked out recipes for aspics and desserts to give away with each package. It was a big success and changed the life of the salesman—Charles B. Knox.

Then there was the young scientist from Brooklyn who in 1914 joined a scientific expedition to Labrador. A fisherman, he cut a hole in the thick arctic ice to try his hand at the sport. The fish he caught froze as soon as they were exposed to the subfreezing air. To his surprise, they could be kept frozen for weeks, then defrosted and cooked like fresh fish without loss of texture or flavor. His name was Charles Birdseye, and he was founder of the first quick-frozen food company.

Looking back at people who have started from a small beginning and have risen to change the world, there seems a certain inevitability about what happened to them. When we hear that it was Birdseye who pulled out that fish that froze, we just know what's going to happen. Heinz's horse-radish grown in the corner of his mother's garden seems more significant than if another boy had done it, because we know what became of Heinz. From our vantage, their obstacles diminish, their opportunities seem better, because we have the assurance that it all worked out. Knowing that, we think that everything was more certain for the great people of "the good old days."

That is just not so. Walk for a minute with W. H. Kellogg over the smoldering remains of his cereal factory. He'd started his business only a year earlier at the age of forty-eight, an age he already suspected was too late in life for such an undertaking. Stocky and balding, wearing a baggy suit, Will Kellogg sniffed the smoky air while others who were milling about wondered what he'd do now that he was virtually wiped out. His employees all expected to be laid off.

Calmly and quietly, though, Kellogg issued instructions. The employees would not lose their jobs; they were to begin cleaning up the mess. An architect from Chicago was immediately summoned, and within twelve hours he was on the job preparing plans for a modern, fireproof factory. Kellogg was knocked down, but he wasn't going to stay down. He had no guarantee that he would succeed; his trials were as pungent as the acrid air, as immediate as an aching back. All he had was courage—plus the will to hang onto his idea, a major cereal factory.

Those who have started from impossibly obscure beginnings and made things possible did not do it just because of the times in which they lived. What seem to us to be the good old days, full of promise, were for them as perilous and uncertain as our own day is for us. They didn't succeed because they had no trials or frustrations or because their triumph was guaranteed at their birth. The time in which we live holds as much opportunity, maybe more, than any other time. There are still frontiers to conquer. Oh, the airplane is flying, the light bulb is screwed into place, the horseless carriage in operation, but the best is yet to be discovered; the best is yet to be invented.

One man writes: "A faucet leaks. I cannot close it tight. Good. I call my seven-year-old son to take another lesson in one of the most important courses I have to teach him. He seizes the faucet, tries to turn it off, can't. He grins.

"'What's the matter, Pete?' I ask.

"He looks up happily, and gives the answer. 'Grownups, Daddy.'

"Propaganda, of course. I have taught him that we, his elders, cannot make a fit faucet. And he may. There's a job for him and his generation in the plumbing business. And in every business.

"I teach my child and I tell other children of all ages—pre-school, in school, in college, and out;

"That nothing is done, finally and right.

"That nothing is known, positively and completely.

"That the world is theirs, all of it. It is full of all sorts of things for them to find out and do, or do over and do right.

"That we have not now and never have had in the history of the world a good government.

"That there is not now and never has been a perfectly run railroad, school, newspaper, bank, factory; that no business is or ever has been built, managed, financed as it should be, must be and will be, someday—possibly in their day.

"That what is true in business and politics is gloriously true of the professions, the arts and crafts, the sciences, the sports. That the best picture has not yet been painted; the greatest poem is still unsung; the mightiest novel remains to be written; the divinest music has not been conceived even by Bach. In science, probably 99 percent of the knowable has to be discovered. We know only a few streaks about astronomy. Chemistry and physics are little more than a sparkling mass of questions. As for the sports, young men and women are beating our old records every year.

"Young people are glad, as I am, that there is something left for them to discover and say and think and do. Something? There is everything." (*Lincoln Steffens Speaking*, New York: Harcourt, Brace Jovanovich, 1936.)

May those of us who live in this day see our opportunities as others have before us.

Learn to Rely
on Yourself

When God created the world, at each stage he stopped for an evaluation, and He called it good. We can well imagine that as He created each individual human being, He did the same, calling His work good.

But a man is sent into the world not as a finality, but as a possibility. We can make of life what we will, and in that sense we have a very real hand in our own creation. We have marvelous, often untapped powers to be the creators of our own personalities and destinies. And it's what we do to finish off what God started that really counts.

Yet many of us are slow to recognize the power we have to shape ourselves. As William George Jordan said, "When a man fails in life he usually says, 'I am as God made me.' When he succeeds he proudly proclaims himself a 'self-made man.'"

A man can be his own best friend as he is a creator of circumstances, directing his possibilities and his responses to life. A man is his own worst enemy as he becomes merely a creature of circumstance, saying it is life that has made him the way he is. He never had a chance.

Yet how easy it is to blame circumstances for what we are. We say things like "It's just bad luck that has done this to

me," or "I'm not appreciated, not recognized," or "I've never
been at the right place at the right time." Something else is
always at fault. We do not want to change ourselves.

But when we voice such attitudes, we are suggesting
that somebody else should take responsibility for us, that we
crawl through life without control, sluggishly susceptible to
whatever pressure or circumstances might happen upon us.
We are merely feeble worms of the dust. Or worse, if we
don't blame circumstances for our plight, we blame the
Lord. He should direct our life and guarantee our successes.
He should not have given us the awful responsibility and
honor of putting us at the helm.

But no one else can unfold our character and therefore
our life. As Jordan also said, "Until a man be truly filled with
the knowledge of the majesty of his possibility, until there
comes to him the glow or realization of his privilege to live
the life committed to him as an individual life for which he is
individually responsible, he is merely groping through the
years."

Can we pass responsibility to the Lord for circumstances of our life and personality? It would be as impossible as what the young man did in the following story.

"I remembered one morning when I discovered a co-
coon in the bark of a tree, just as the butterfly was making a
hole in its case and preparing to come out. I waited a while,
but it was too long appearing and I was impatient. I bent
over it and breathed on it to warm it. I warmed it as quickly
as I could and the miracle began to happen before my eyes,
faster than life. The case opened, the butterfly started slowly
crawling out and I shall never forget my horror when I saw
how its wings were folded back and crumpled; the wretched
butterfly tried with its whole trembling body to unfold them.
Bending over it, I tried to help it with my breath. In vain. It
needed to hatch out patiently and the unfolding of the wings

should be a gradual process in the sun. Now it was too late. My breath had forced the butterfly to appear, all crumpled, before its time. It struggled desperately and, a few seconds later, died in the palm of my hand." (Nikos Kazantzakis, *Zorba the Greek*, New York: Simon and Schuster, 1952, pp. 120-21.)

Like the young man with the butterfly, the Lord will not do for us what we were meant to do for ourselves. There must finally come a time in every life when one learns that "no one can realize my possibilities for me but me: no one can make me good or evil but myself." On that day we finally learn self-reliance; we finally learn that the control center of our existence, the still point of our turning world, is in ourselves and not someplace else.

We've often heard the aphorism, "The Lord helps those who help themselves." Knute Rockne applied this principle to football when he said, "Prayers work best when players are big."

In fact, existence for each of us may be summed up by what a minister told a farmer who called him in to pray for better crops. After looking over the stony, barren soil, the minister said, "This farm doesn't need prayer—what this farm needs is manure!"

A person's life is not run by a committee in which he has to vote. It is an individual journey, and he has ultimate control if he will but recognize it. If he is patient, it is because he decided to have many small victories of character in the face of frustration. He did not say, "*You* made me angry. *You* made me yell." If he is well-read, it is not because he sent a friend to the library and watched that friend read. He himself spent the hours in concentration, searching humanity's great ideas. If he is physically fit, he did not send a servant to the gym. He exerted the muscles himself.

Jordan said, "Life is an individual problem that man

must solve for himself. Nature accepts no vicarious service. Nature never recognizes a proxy vote. She has nothing to do with middlemen—she deals only with the individual. Nature is constantly seeking to show man that he is his own best friend or his own worst enemy."

The day, then, that we finally realize that we are in control is the day we finally ought to take control, refusing to surrender to weaknesses, bad habits, or false passions. We don't have to accept blindly our present condition and live forever with the character flaws that dismay us. We are in control, so let us take control.

Do we envy another for his gifts, his fortune, his family? No, we follow the process by which he achieved them.

We can fulfill our most marvelous dreams and live nearer the limits of our possibilities if we will assume the reins and quit blaming others for what happens. But if we will be self-reliant, we must have self-control. Those who are victors instead of victims of this existence have learned to pay the price. The price is not exacted in one large payment, one grand effort. That would be too easy. Instead the payment is in many small installments, consistently made day after day. We gain control of our destiny by first gaining control of our minutes, just as musicians learn to play an instrument with daily practice, not in one intense session.

The soul who can rise above his circumstances and determine his life is the one who can rise above them minute by minute. The one who can create a new character is one who can in small victories overcome his weaknesses—getting up when he'd really rather stay in bed, working when he'd rather rest, being patient when he'd rather snarl.

The Lord created us and called us good. As we continue that creation every day, may we be able to give the same evaluation.

Jesus' Example
of Constancy

If you ever wanted to understand the meaning of constancy, you only need to explore the last few hours of the life of Jesus Christ. He was a constant in an inconstant world as His enemies plotted against Him, and His friends one by one succumbed to their human weaknesses. In His hour of greatest need, He was utterly alone.

Perhaps you might think that a lifetime of rejection had prepared Him for His last desperate hours. "Will ye also go away?" He plaintively asked of His apostles, as others were turning from Him earlier in His life. (John 6:67.) He had been homeless, taunted by His own, with the leaders of His people seeking to trap Him at every turn. But nothing was like the end.

Think about it. The end began with His triumphal ride into Jerusalem on the back of a donkey. It was the time of Passover, and Jerusalem was teeming with visitors who had come for their holy festival. The common people were interested in every act and movement of the Master. They were jubilant as He rode into the city, and they spread out their garments and cast palm fronds and other foliage in His path. For the time being he was their King and they, His adoring subjects. Where was this crowd just days later when He walked up the same streets, degraded, carrying a cross? Their shouts of praise had vanished on the night wind, their love grown cold. How inconstant man can be!

But it wasn't the crowds alone who left Him. Bit by bit He was deserted by every trapping of this mortal world, every friend who had benefitted from His love.

The Last Supper, of course, was a time of communion and commitment between the Lord and His apostles. Then, together, they traveled to the Garden of Gethsemane. Leaving most of the apostles at the entrance to the garden, He took Peter, James, and John further in. Knowing the agony that was before Him, when he would take upon Himself the sins of all the world, He "began to be sore amazed, and to be very heavy." (Mark 14:33.) He begged of his chosen three, "My soul is exceeding sorrowful, even unto death; tarry ye here, and watch with me." (Matthew 26:38.) His plea was twofold. He needed someone to watch for those who would soon come to bind Him and take Him away to an unfair judgment, and He needed someone to be there during the hour of His deepest humiliation and profound anguish.

The apostles had good intentions, of course, but they fell asleep despite his plea. Again the Lord came out to them. Addressing Peter, who so short a time before had loudly proclaimed his readiness to follow the Lord even to prison and death, He said, "What, could ye not watch with me one hour?" Aroused, the apostles watched the Lord retreat again to His agony, and once more they fell asleep. When for the last time Jesus came out to check on His apostles, He found them again slumbering. He knew it was no use to rouse His companions again, so He simply said, "Sleep on now, and take your rest: behold, the hour is at hand, and the Son of man is betrayed into the hands of sinners." (Matthew 26:40, 45.)

Elder James Talmage described what Christ was facing

in the garden: "Christ's agony in the garden is unfathomable by the finite mind, both as to intensity and cause. The thought that He suffered through fear of death is untenable. . . . He struggled and groaned under a burden such as no other being who has lived on earth might conceive as possible. It was not physical pain, nor mental anguish alone . . . but a spiritual agony of soul as only God was capable of experiencing." (*Jesus the Christ*, Salt Lake City: Deseret Book, 1973, p. 613.) He was bearing, in brutal intensity, the sins of all the world. But His loyal three could not even stay awake.

When the band of Roman soldiers finally arrived at the garden, they were led by one of Christ's own Twelve, Judas, and the sign of betrayal was a kiss. How much more painful it must have been for the Lord to be betrayed by one who had walked with Him and feigned devotion than to be betrayed by a misunderstanding enemy, to be betrayed by a kiss instead of a slap.

Christ, bound and captive, was taken next to a night meeting of the Sanhedrin, composed of the chief priests, scribes, and elders of the Jewish people. Thirsty for His blood, they charged Him with blasphemy. How ironic, to accuse Christ, Jehovah Himself, of blaspheming Jehovah. Oh, how the law deserted Him during this mock trial! They had unlawfully caused Jesus to be arrested at night; they couldn't find two corroborating witnesses, though that was a strict necessity; and they compelled Christ to testify against Himself. On and on marched the illegalities, as Christ patiently submitted to it all, constant in forbearance against the inconstancy of the law.

Peter, the impulsive disciple who was always so quick to swear allegiance to the Lord, grew frightened as he sat outside the palace during the proceedings. Recognized as a follower of Christ, he vehemently denied it. "I know not this man of whom ye speak," he cried. Asked again, he denied again. When he was confronted a third time, he again denied that he knew the Lord. And then, we are told, "he went out, and wept bitterly." (Matthew 26:69-75; Mark 14:66-72.)

To get the death penalty for which they sought, the council sent Christ to the Roman official Pilate, early the next morning. Pilate said he could see no fault in the man; three different times he proclaimed Christ's innocence. The Sanhedrin came back each time and demanded Christ's death, threatening Pilate if he did not comply. Pilate deserted his sense of justice at the steady demands, "Crucify him, crucify him." He finally muttered, "Take ye him, and crucify him: I find no fault in him." (John 19:6.)

Jesus submitted to scourging and being crowned with a ring of thorns, as those around Him deserted their sense of decency. "Hail, King of the Jews!" they laughed as they hit Him with their hands and spat upon Him. (Mark 15:17-19; John 19:1-3.)

With His apostles scattered and frightened, the adoring crowds of yesterday vanished, the Lord, weakened with His ordeal, carried His own cross much of the way to Calvary. Though some women called out to Him in pity along the way, not a man gave comfort or admitted discipleship.

Death by crucifixion was one of the most lingering and painful forms of execution, as sensitive nerves were crushed and pain was unremitting. But most painful were the taunts of those around Him, "If thou be the king of the Jews, save thyself." (Luke 23:37.) That mocking *if* was sent at this last moment perhaps to make Christ question His own identity, to doubt himself.

So the last hours of Christ's life are a lesson in constancy. The actions of those around him show how inconstant man can be when he's under pressure and frightened by a world that is too big for him. We see how inconstant standards, laws, and even the supposedly best institutions of man can be. But through these long hours we do see one constant, the Lord Himself. He was and is undeviating in His word and His love.

Jesus taught the people that when He died, He would rise again on the third day. And when Mary and others went to His tomb, bearing spices to embalm the body, they found instead an empty cave and two angels, who told them, "He is not here: for he is risen." (Matthew 28:6.) The message was almost too good for His followers to believe. They were incredulous, though they had been told. In an uncertain, dark world, there was certainty, there was promise, and it came, as it always had, from the Lord Jesus Christ. Though He had been deserted by all, He would not desert His promise.

For each of us, there are times when the inconstancy of this world seems almost overwhelming, with promises not kept, dreams not fulfilled. Perhaps we feel that most when we lose a loved one in death. How can someone who was so much a part of our lives be suddenly gone? What was the use of trying so hard? It is then that we need to remember that the Lord will not desert us. Despite all momentary appearances, He is as good as His word. He said He would rise, and He did. He said He will be there for us, and He will. It is His constancy that marks Him from every other being or institution in this world. Though He was deserted, He will not desert us.

You Are Still
Being Created

The English teacher, a big bear of a man with a shock of wavy white hair, looked down at the young man in his class. The student opened his looseleaf binder and began hesitantly to read. It was a composition of his own, though not of his own choosing. The class had been assigned to write a poem in the style of the eminent English poet Alexander Pope.

The young man had the dubious honor of being chosen to read aloud his offering. He fervently wished that his bit of poetry could be dropped into the depths of the sea or blasted into outer space. But the professor was not a man to be trifled with, so the young man began to read. He managed a sentence or two, then stumbled, halted, put down the book, and blurted out in frustration, "I can't do this. I am not a poet."

There was an ominous silence. Then storm clouds gathered in the teacher's big face. Nothing the student could have said short of "the school building is on fire!" could have triggered such an explosion from that volatile, demanding, and absolutely marvelous English teacher. "Young man," he roared from behind his desk. "Never let me hear you say that again!" His eyes bored deeply into the eyes and the soul of that student and of every student in the class. His words were slow and measured, distinct and final. He said, "You do not know what you are and what you may become. You are still being created!"

It was an electric teaching moment, one that was indelibly engraved in the mind of every person in that class. "You are still being created" probably echoes yet in their memories, though the words were spoken decades ago.

Recently I passed a desk piled high with papers, and behind it a young woman was hastily riffling through the stacks, doing her best to complete her day's work. She was obviously under some pressure, but the little sign on her desk put the whole thing into perspective for me. It read "Be patient. God is not finished with me yet."

It is important to realize that you are constantly in a state of becoming. You are not the same person today that you were yesterday, and you will not be the same tomorrow. For better or for worse, you are constantly being changed and renewed. The body regenerates one billion red blood cells every day; your head grows twenty-five feet of hair in an average lifetime. In the course of a few weeks, your entire layer of skin is replaced.

Likewise, in the inner rooms of your mind you are constantly changing the decor and the furniture as you add new experiences, new ideas. You cannot help having new things coming into your mind as long as you are alive.

There is nothing in this world so constant as is change, particularly change in people. Sometimes people resist this changing in themselves or in those about them. It is unsettling to have to constantly deal with the new and the unusual when the old and tried, the comfortable and familiar would be so much easier. But that is the nature of life, and thank goodness for it.

Thank goodness for optimism such as I once saw in a

fourteen-year-old girl. She was writing down her daily list of things to do, including cleaning her room, completing her English assignment, and shopping for a new sweater. Down the list, somewhere around number seven or eight, she wrote, "Get a new personality." Well now, setting out to get a new personality might be a bit ambitious for one afternoon's work, but she is on the right track, and with that kind of confidence and desire, she can get a new personality or virtually anything else she wants in life.

Each of us is constantly growing and changing. What is important, vitally important, eternally and everlastingly important, is, what direction are you going in? Where is the constant change in your life taking you? Are you better today than you were yesterday, and will you be better tomorrow than you are today? If not, then the irrevocable law of change will eventually take you and make you what you would not like to be.

But if you are improving, even ever so slowly, even haltingly, even two steps forward and one step back, but in the balance coming out with a net gain in your progress, then you may be at peace knowing that you will eventually arrive at your chosen destination. You may safely bury your old self with each sundown and know that each sunrise is your birthday, the first day of the rest of your life.

With each rising sun and with each passing hour and minute, you are constantly being created. The challenge is to keep going and not get discouraged. As a matter of fact, the young man who was trying to write a poem like Alexander Pope would have gotten some comfort from reading what that wise old gentleman wrote about growing and becoming:

Not to go back is somewhat to advance,
And men must walk, at least, before they dance.

Your Amazing Mind

At this very moment, far into the outer reaches of our solar system, a small, intrepid little piece of machinery is shooting through space at thousands of miles per hour. It has gone beyond the known planets and is destined to sail on beyond our system. So far as we know, it will never return.

This incredible space probe has gone deep into the vast frontiers of space. It has sent back spectacular pictures and reams of data for computer analysis. It has already made some theory-shaking discoveries. The farther it goes, the more it seems that our universe is infinite and filled with amazing and varied kinds of things. It is an exciting and a humbling experience to probe the universe.

On the other end of this historic exploration is another universe, one that is equally deep, profound, and thus far unfathomable. It is a universe with far-flung frontiers even more exciting than the distant reaches of space. This intriguing universe is the minds of the men and women who dreamed, planned, constructed, and launched this space probe.

The same sorts of human minds have created or discovered everything we know about the universe and this earth. They have put human beings on the moon. They have discovered how to cure and eradicate some of the most dreaded diseases. They have established governments and built civilizations where there was wilderness, created art out of disorganized sounds, lines, colors, and movements. They have developed complex signals for speech and writing and mathematics. They have learned to think abstractly and symbolically.

The mind that is properly developed and used is without question the most amazing object yet discovered in the whole universe. I hope it is exciting to you to know that you own one of these incredible computers free and clear. And it is yours. No one has the right to take it from you or to force it in some direction against your will. It is also your privilege and responsibility to develop your mind, fill it with the right thoughts, and use it for good and worthy purposes.

Your brain is a deceptively insignificant-looking organ. It begins life looking quite similar to the brain of a gorilla, but then the human brain triples in size the first year, growing unlike anything else known in the animal world. But even so, the size never gets spectacular. In fact, one of the incredible things about the brain is that "two fistfuls of pink-gray tissue, wrinkled like a walnut, [can] store more information than all the libraries of the world." (Richard M. Restak, "The Brain," *The Wilson Quarterly,* Summer 1982, p. 114.)

Medical science is, by its own admission, just scratching the surface in understanding the brain's capabilities. The ancients had various theories about the brain. Aristotle and the Greeks thought it was a radiator system for cooling the blood. The ancient Egyptians considered it relatively useless. They theorized that the heart area was the center of intelligence for humans.

In our day the brain has been compared to a great computer. In some ways this is accurate, but in other ways the brain goes far beyond the abilities of the most intelligent computer. It has incredible storage capacity, as does a large computer. In your subconscious mind is stored all the information you have ever been exposed to. Every whisper you have heard, every glance of the eye, every feeling taken in by your senses, and perhaps much that you're not aware of, is stored indelibly in your subconscious mind.

While a person may seem unable to bring these scenes to the conscious mind at will, that apparently is a limitation of the recall and playback system, not the storage capacity. During the 1950s Wilder Penfield, a Canadian neurosurgeon, and his colleagues made a startling discovery. They used tiny electrical probes to touch parts of an exposed brain, and whole scenes immediately unfolded in the mind of the subject, full-color reenactments of previous experiences, complete with sound, smells, and feelings. The scenes appeared to be not so much remembered as relived in the memory.

Apparently the recall system has been somewhat selective. Otherwise each of us would be constantly swimming in a sea of past scenes and memories that might keep us from functioning effectively in the present. But all the information we have ever learned is with us, still molding and shaping our thoughts and our characters. Thus it would behoove us to try and fill our minds only with the things we really want to keep.

The mind has been compared to a gigantic switchboard, with messages constantly coming in and going out. Again, in some ways this analogy is accurate; in other ways it is insufficient. Small electrical impulses carry messages to the brain and then back out to the body, but chemical changes are also taking place. Waves, moods, and fluctuations go beyond the mere summing up of the electrical messages sent. There is more going on than just a human switchboard here.

There is much we don't know about the brain and the mind, but there are some things we do know because of research and revelation from Him who created us. We know that the mind and soul of man is the most valuable creation in all the universe. We know that with guidance from God, the human mind has the capacity to eventually search out all secrets and the capability to solve all the problems with which the world is beset.

We know that beyond all the electrical impulses, the mental waves, and the chemical changes that make the brain physically work, there is an essence and ability to think, to feel, to understand, to emphasize, to care for and to love one another. We know that we each have free agency to decide our course and follow it. Jesus said, "If the son therefore shall make you free, ye shall be free indeed." (John 8:36.) There is also in the mind a whispering that tells us not to despair, that the magnificent mind we own is eternal, immortal, and shall not pass away.

These are the most important things that your mind can tell you if you will listen.

Learn to Receive Graciously

There is an awkward streak in human nature that makes it hard for us to receive. Whether it be instruction, a compliment, a service, or even a gift, we often squirm when we are on the receiving end.

Take instruction, for example. One of the first signs that a two-year-old is beginning to be his own person is when he plants his feet squatly and announces "I'll do it myself." Teenagers often believe they know all things, and they'll turn deaf ears to their parents' best counsel. Like the two-year-old and the teenager, most of us dislike advice. We'd often rather make our own mistakes than let someone tell us how to avoid them.

Do you know any good receivers? Watch what most people do when given a compliment. They long for words of praise and do plenty of back-breaking, head-knocking work to earn them, but when someone actually acknowledges their strengths, they begin to feel uncomfortable. Faced with a compliment, they first deny it, saying something like, "Oh, my work on this job? Anyone could have done it," or "You like this old dress? I just picked it up at a garage sale for five dollars." And if they can't deny it, they hurriedly throw the compliment back like a catcher tossing back a hot pitch.

Consider how loath people are to acknowledge their need for the services of others. They hate to admit their weaknesses or vulnerabilities, and often they are reluctant to put others out by asking for help even when they really need it. One woman who had had surgery at the hospital came home on a bus, standing and waiting at the bus stop for half an hour, enduring a long ride home with many stops, and then walking with great difficulty the last blocks to her apartment—all to avoid putting someone out by asking for a ride.

Yes, it may be more blessed to give than it is to receive, but it is also a lot easier. The reason for this is probably because when any of us is the giver, we are operating from a position of strength. We are acknowledging to ourselves and to the world that our cup is full enough to overflow. Needy? No, *we* can fill needs. Insufficient? *We* are sufficient enough to even serve others. There is joy in giving, and there is joy in knowing we are strong enough to give.

On the other hand, when we receive instruction, compliments, or services, we may have the subtle feeling that we are slightly inferior, that we have a need so obvious that someone can recognize and fill it. We may feel that we are incomplete, a puzzle without all the pieces. If someone can teach us something, if someone can give us something, we may interpret it to mean that we have not been sufficient to fill our own needs, that we are not independent, invulnerable powerhouses. And too many of us suffer from false pride, believing that it is a terrible weakness to admit dependency on others or ignorance of certain things.

Yet the truth is, we are all in need, we are all dependent, we are all ignorant in certain areas. We were not created to stride the earth with mighty, proud steps, insulated from others by our stiff independence. The life span itself teaches us that. We are born as infants, dependent for every meal and every comfort from a stronger hand. Then, as we approach old age, once more our steps are faltering and we need the secure arms of others to hold us up. Between those two extremes, we benefit from the collected knowledge of millions who have gone before us, filled because of a network of people who grow, transport, and distribute food, surviving because of a layer of top soil and a few inches of rainfall.

As Will and Ariel Durant have written, "A tornado can ruin in an hour the city that took a century to build; an iceberg can overturn or bisect the floating palace and send a thousand merrymakers gurgling to the Great Certainty. Let rain become too rare, and civilization disappears under sand as in Central Asia; let it fall too furiously, and civilization will be choked with jungle, as in Central America." (*The Lessons of History*, New York: Simon and Schuster, 1968, p. 15.)

Human life is tenuous, and we flourish only because of our ability to depend on each other and the gifts of a usually benevolent nature. Are we receivers, then? Yes. Every minute of our lives we are given more gifts than we can count, services from those who may never know they have served. Do we need to accept instruction? Yes. There was never a person who didn't need to be taught at least the basics to survive. To see humanity with any clarity is to see us as receivers, dependent on each other and the Lord.

Now, I point this out not to make us feel servile or helpless, but to make us feel grateful. It reminds me of the story of the man who reportedly stood before a masterful painting and said, "I can see nothing in it." The great artist replied, "Don't you wish you could?" When life seems sparse and tight-fisted, when it seems we have been given nothing but frustration and obstacles, when we are, in fact, tempted to say with the man in front of the marvelous painting, "I can see nothing in it," we may need to remember the words of the artist, "Don't you wish you could?"

And beyond that, when we feel ourselves take that proud pose that suggests no one can help us or teach us, we need to let down the stance and to become willing to learn from others and accept their services without a high-handed show of total knowledge. Plain, uncomplicated acceptance is the nicest thing any of us can do for a giver.

Michael Drury tells the story of a movie executive who once gave her secretary a check for $25 at Christmas and apologized that is was not a more thoughtful gift. She said she just hadn't had time to shop.

"The secretary smiled and said, 'Wow! You don't know what a relief that is to me. I'm in exactly the same position, and I'd been wondering how to offer you this.' Then she handed her boss a check for $5.

"Instantly the woman backed away and went into a long speech about what the secretary could afford, how she—the employer—could have deducted $5 from her own check if that was what she intended. The secretary listened quietly, then said, 'You've been a wonderful employer, and you've taught me 90 percent of what I know. But there's one thing I can teach you: learn to accept. It's more fun for everybody that way.'

"Stunned, the woman finally replied, 'You're right. May I have that check? There are some expensive stockings I've been wanting, and I thank you very much.'" ("How to Say Thank You," *Reader's Digest*, July 1963, p. 175.)

Becoming a gracious receiver may be an art each of us has to learn, but it is essential to the mature human character. Two-year-olds may proudly announce that they'll do it themselves, but as we grow, we simply ought to know better. We can't do it ourselves, and there is no use trying. Every day we receive gifts of instruction and service. Some days we receive compliments. But always, those who recognize that dependence on each other is a rule of life will let haughtiness fade away and will find joy in being gracious receivers.

Be a Well-Rounded Square

I was walking down the hall of a big health clinic recently. On the doors of the offices I read the names of all the medical specialists: ophthalmologists, cardiologists, dermatologists, and a lot of "ologists" that I could hardly pronounce, much less know the meaning of. Skin, bones, eyes, ears, noses, and throats—the doctors had pretty well divided up our bodies among their various specialties. I half expected to see a specialist for left ears in one office, and one for right ears across the hall. Maybe there was—I'm not sure.

A few days later I glanced at the magazine rack in a bookstore, and I had a similiar impression. Many of the old general-interest magazines are gone, and in their place, specialty magazines filled the shelves: publications for people who like cars, or houses, or collecting coins. This is the trend in the publishing business, I'm told, and the number of specialty magazines grows every year.

Some of the same things are happening in scientific and academic fields. The explosion of knowledge has forced researchers to limit themselves to ever-narrowing fields of expertise. A friend who is a college professor said he is now learning more and more about less and less. He laughed and added, "If this keeps up, I may someday know everything about nothing." And even in sports, if they need a punt or an extra point on the football field, they call in a specialist.

We do live in an age of specialization. It's easy to see some of the reasons why. Much of our world is so complicated and technical that it takes specialists in a thousand fields working together to make the whole thing go. None of us know enough about the whole picture that we could survive on our own on anything higher than a subsistence existence.

So when we get sick, we go to the medical specialist. When our car breaks down, we go to the front-end or the transmission or tune-up specialist, and when we have to punt the football, we call in the kicking specialists.

Likewise, if we are to make a contribution to the world, we need to pick out certain areas that we are adapted to, and develop and fine-tune our talents in that area so that we can add to the collective skill and expertise of the human race.

Specializing has given us incredibly well-trained and talented people and provided our society with necessities and comforts we would not have otherwise enjoyed. So in this specialized world, we will always find ourselves relying on the experts. In our own personal world, however, it is a different matter. In the world of our own development, we ourselves need to become the experts. We can call in specialists for help, but we can't hire or commission anyone to do our developing for us.

And we ought to be a bit general in our approach here as well. Each of us needs certain skills of body, mind, and spirit if we are to successfully negotiate our journey through this life. We need to be well rounded in our development, and square and honest with ourselves and others. We might call it becoming a well-rounded square.

The perfect example of the well-developed life was Jesus. The Bible doesn't tell us much about how He grew to the stature of manhood, but in one short verse it does give us a valuable glimpse. Speaking of his boyhood, Luke states, "And Jesus increased in wisdom and stature, and in favour with God and man." (Luke 2:52.)

Wisdom, stature, God and man. Let's take a look at each of these.

How did He get wisdom? We see some clues in His life. As a young boy, He was found in the temple talking with the wise ones, the "doctors" of His people. We have sometimes interpreted that scene incorrectly. We usually picture a young prodigy instructing and amazing his audience of elders and pouring out information far beyond his years. But the Bible doesn't say that. It says He was there "both hearing them, and asking them questions." (Luke 2:46.) Later on in His ministry, in the midst of discussion and debates, He frequently called up examples from the history and the law of the people with whom He was speaking. He was well acquainted with their scholarly works, even though He came from a relatively humble household.

He grew in stature, strong of body. He was a carpenter, which in those days meant hewing the timbers by hand and hoisting heavy beams up to walls and ceilings. It was hard work, but He knew his trade, and He did it well.

He grew in favor with God. He fasted, prayed, spoke to His Father in Heaven, and conformed His life to the will of God as He received it through prayer. Jesus had the quiet confidence of knowing, even as a boy, that He was about his "Father's business."

And Jesus increased in favor with man. Some of the prudish people of His day criticized Him because He was so popular. He was welcome at weddings, feasts, and dinners. He knew the priceless power of a word or gesture of encouragement, a sincere compliment. He called the sinners to repentance when necessary, but he seemed to prefer the quiet and gentle way whenever that would work. He told the woman taken in adultery that He did not condemn her. He invited the hated tax collector to join His company, and He ministered to the outcast lepers whom others considered unclean. He loved people; even on the cross He prayed for His Father to forgive them. And those about Him loved Him in return as a treasured and trusted friend.

We would do well to look at our own lives and ask ourselves, are we developing our bodies and our minds, our friendship and kindness to others, and our relationship with the Lord? Are we taking a well-rounded and four-square approach to becoming the best persons we can be? If not, let's pick up the slack in those parts of our personality that are falling behind in development, and become well-rounded squares.

Born to Win

The official scorekeeper was taking the names of the athletes for the track meet. "Hey, we're about to start," he said. "Where's your team?"

"Right here," replied a smiling young man.

The scorekeeper put down his pencil and looked up questioningly. "Lafayette College has 48 men on their track team. Are you telling me you two guys are the whole team from your school?"

The young man replied, "Oh, no. We're not the whole team. I'm the whole team. He's the team manager."

That day this one-man team won the high jump, broad jump, shotput, discus, 120-yard hurdles, and 220-yard hurdles, and finished third in the 100-yard dash. He won the track meet 71 to 41.

This same quiet young man was just about the whole football team too, when little Carlisle Indian School upset mighty Harvard. That day he kicked four field goals and scored a touchdown. In another game, against a very good Army team, he ran for two touchdowns, passed for another one, and kicked three extra points and three field goals. He returned an Army kick 90 yards for a touchdown, but it was called back by a penalty; on the next kickoff, he ran 95 yards for another touchdown.

This one-man team, this all-around everything on the athletic field, was the immortal Jim Thorpe. In track and field events, he excelled in almost every event. On the grid-iron he could pass and run, and he could punt the football 70 yards.

But to me, the most inspirational side of Jim Thorpe was not his incredible athletic ability. It was his indomitable spirit. Jim was the kind of guy who never bothered to ask what the chances of success were. He just went out and gave it his best shot, which often was enough to win the day against overwhelming odds.

Let's talk about that individual effort and will to win for a minute. What has happened to it?

Since Jim Thorpe's day, we've become very adept and sophisticated about determining the chances of success. No great- or even medium-size endeavor of modern man could possibly be launched today without feasibility studies. How else could one interest the investors, collect the capital, persuade the public, beguile the buyers, and everything else it takes to get an enterprise off the ground?

Now I'm all for taking careful calculations, but I'm also aware that most of the greatest accomplishments of mankind would look less than promising in a feasibility study. One can only speculate how bleak the prospects would have been for the man who wanted to sail three tiny ships to the East Indies by heading west. But fortunately for us, Christopher Columbus decided to try it anyway.

And what about the thirteen tiny colonies that proclaimed their independence against the world's greatest military power in 1776? The smart money would have picked them to be squashed like a bug under the English heel.

Who would have invested capital or confidence in those eleven men two thousand years ago who, from a backwater town on the outskirts of the Roman Empire, set out boldly to preach the gospel of Jesus Christ to every nation, kindred, tongue, and people? Though they were harassed, oppressed, and opposed by the mightiest civilization the world had ever seen, yet they succeeded in changing the face of the world and bringing hope to millions.

These and a multitude of other accomplishments throughout history suggest that more of our limitations are in our own minds and hearts than in the conditions in which we find ourselves. I am not suggesting that we ought to fanatically follow every will-o'-the-wisp idea that strikes our fancy, but I am reminded that when people believe strongly enough in what they are doing, take the responsibility for their part in the project, and give it all they've got, they can throw the odds-makers' charts out the window.

Rudyard Kipling, in the poem "If," penned these noble lines that we don't hear so much anymore:

> *If you can keep your head while all about you*
> *Are losing theirs and blaming it on you;*
> *If you can trust yourself when all men doubt you*
> *But make allowance for their doubting too; . . .*
> *If you can fill the unforgiving minute*
> *With sixty seconds' worth of distance run—*
> *Yours is the Earth and everything that's in it,*
> *And—which is more—you'll be a Man, my son.*

Oh, how we need men and women like that in today's world. We have become very adept at explaining why things can't work or won't work; then we go forth and fulfill our own prophecies, rationalizing the reasons for failure, mediocrity, and substandard performance. We blame environment, heredity, preconditioning, lack of motivation. We have a hundred reasons for explaining why things didn't turn out as well as we had hoped, but none of them are as good or as satisfying as the success would have been.

We were not born to lose. We were born to win, not through ignoble or unfair tactics, and not through conquering others, but by conquering ourselves. Elbert Hubbard put it this way, "Some men succeed by what they know; some by what they do; and a few by what they are."

This is the real struggle for success that each of us must face, the battle to be our best. That is the arena of life in which we must excel no matter what the odds against us. And we can, for we have within us gifts that can be developed into greatness. We have the seeds of success sprouting within our souls. We have the royal blood of champions in our veins. Each of us is a child of God, and as such, we have unlimited abilities.

The greatest joys of life will come as we overcome all opposition and turn our potential into reality.

Is Anything Too Hard for the Lord?

A group of people standing on the bank of a wide river were surprised to look up and see a man in a business suit racing down the hill toward the bank, hollering, "Gangway! Look out!" They moved aside as he zoomed past them, hit the edge of the bank, sprang out as far as he could, and splashed into the water. He bubbled beneath the surface for a moment, then popped up and waded back to shore. His suit was dripping and disheveled, his briefcase spewed out a couple of fish, but he was undaunted.

The amazed onlookers asked him, "Just exactly what were you doing?"

"Well," the man replied, "A friend of mine bet me a thousand dollars that I couldn't jump across this river, and with odds like that, I just couldn't resist the impulse to at least try."

That's a delightful story that radio commentator Earl Nightingale tells. It is the amusing view of an irrepressible optimist who just had to give it his best shot, no matter what the chances of success. Of course, his approach was a little reckless, foolhardy, and waterlogged. He would have been better off to hike to the headwaters of the river. There he could have jumped it with an easy leap, won his bet, and probably had enough money to ride back in style.

But at least he tried, and that's more than many do. Too

often we just sit gazing at the water, wishing we were on the other side, but afraid to get our feet wet. We will never be laughed at; we will never be dripping and defeated. But neither will we feel the thrill of effort and the greater thrill of victory.

The man who attempted to leap the river was hardly more audacious than the two New England bicycle makers who tried to fly, or the wild-haired physicist with a blackboard and a piece of chalk who tried to catch the atomic power of the sun in a mathematical formula, or the intrepid Italian who sailed west to get to the east, with the edge of the world and the yawning chasms of nothingness and sea monsters between him and success.

They were all a little crazy to the cautious crowd that looked on. But the Wright brothers, Albert Einstein, and Christopher Columbus all looked directly at impossibility and said, "Let's give it a try."

Do you have some secret, pent-up desire deep inside you that you're afraid to admit even to yourself for fear someone might laugh or criticize or condemn you? If you do, you are like most of us. Furthermore, if you are like too many of us, you have been working hard on that dream—working hard, but in the wrong direction.

Many of us chisel out blocks—solid, firm blocks that could be the foundation and walls and soaring towers of our castle in the sky. But instead of building a mansion, we build walls between ourselves and the person we would like to be or the things we would like to accomplish. We make a magnificent piece of construction—but with each block a carefully considered reason why we can't succeed. Along the top we put a row of spikes to show how painful it would be to be impaled by our own imagination.

Often we paint the whole thing with a glossy coat of excuses that will look good to us and to others. Sometimes we even insulate our walls to keep the fires of our enthusiasm from giving a hot seat to our apathy. Then for good measure we spread a protective row of stumbling blocks around, stumbling blocks that could have been used as stepping-stones.

Sometimes we spend a lifetime just building and maintaining the walls between us and what we would like to be. The pity is that with the same effort, we could be training ourselves to leap over our obstacles. Or if we couldn't make it with a single Supermanlike bound, we could at least learn to inch and claw and climb our way over our self-constructed walls of limitations.

Robert Frost had some profound things to say about walls. He was talking about the walls that divide people, but the same holds true for the walls that separate us from our potential. He wrote, "Before I built a wall I'd ask to know / What I was walling in or walling out." ("Mending Walls.")

What are we walling in or walling out with our walls of apprehension and self-doubt? Are we shutting off our possibilities and limiting our world?

George Santayana said, "Knowledge of what is possible is the beginning of happiness." What is it, then, that keeps us from this knowledge of what is possible? There are a number of things, but I'd like to discuss two of the most common ones I see.

The first is the strange value we put on the status quo. We seem to think there is virtue in being the same person today that we were yesterday, and the same tomorrow. We seem afraid to change. Emerson said we suffer from a "terror that scares us from self-trust." We have, as he said, "a reverence for our past act or word because the eyes of others have no other data for computing our orbit than our past acts, and we are loath to disappoint them. . . . But," he added, "why should you keep your head over your shoulder? Why drag about this corpse of your memory? . . . Suppose you should contradict yourself; what then?" ("Self-reliance.")

What indeed? I suppose it might do us great good to see a new person pop out of the stodgy old habits we've been dragging along in the name of consistency if that consistency has been dragging us down.

A second challenge we face when we try to imagine our possibilities is the chain of practicality we forge for ourselves. "What is it worth?" we ask. What is the bottom line? The payback? Now I'm not suggesting that we should spend our days chasing will-o'-the-wisps. We must, of course, consider costs and benefits in anything we attempt. But to let this be the limit of our dreams is to exclude, ignore, and reject one of the greatest gifts of the Lord—the power to imagine ourselves not as we are, but as we could be.

Among the great lessons of the Bible, none are more important than this. The pages are filled with so-called practical people who had to be shown their possibilities: Gideon, whose tiny strike force of three hundred beat the whole Midianite army; little David, who slew the giant Goliath; little Israel, which stood up against the empires of those days; the twelve apostles who stood up against the world.

The story of the aged Abraham gives us the most meaningful question we can ask ourselves about any endeavor. Though he was told he would have a son, he knew that his wife was far beyond childbearing years, and that she had always been barren. But the messenger who came to Abraham said simply, "Is any thing too hard for the Lord?" (Genesis 18:14.)

That is really the relevant question. Not how broad is the river, how tough is the task, how impossible are the odds, how capable are we, but is it something that needs to be done for good and righteous reasons? Would you have the Lord's approval and benediction on our work? If so, take heart and ask yourself, "Is anything too hard for the Lord?"

What You Do Makes
a Difference

There are seven words you ought never to use—at least not use together. It's not because they are ungrammatical; they would pass any English teacher's muster. It's not even that they are innately offensive; we use each word hundreds of times every day. It is when we use them together that they become one of the most devastating sentences in the human language.

What are those seven words? Simply this: "What I do doesn't make any difference."

Probably very few of us haven't felt that way at one time or another. When you give your best and no one seems to care, when you wonder if you have any worth as a human being, when you never seem to arrive at that time when life is without its frustrations and adjustments, then is the time that thought comes creeping into your heart—"What I do doesn't make any difference." That is the time when you just don't want to try anymore, the time when you look around and see a world of needs, and you doubt that you can do anything that will matter.

But pause a moment. Think back on your life. Haven't you been greatly helped by someone? Haven't you been helped "by a parent whose concern and continuing care shaped your character, by a teacher who was enough of a friend to show you how to continue when you were ready to give up, by an employer whose awareness of your talents opened the way for your success, by a neighbor whose respect for you and your family made you feel at home where you live—perhaps by a stranger whose unexpected help came just when you needed it?" (Bernard Mandelbaum and Victor M. Ratner, "The Excuse We Should Never Use," *Reader's Digest*, December 1963, p. 79.)

Knowing that these people made such a difference in your life, isn't it clear that you can do that also whenever your life touches someone else? You can be the one to lift a dark day, to make the world seem less lonely, to add a little bit of security in an insecure world.

Living in a world where the media make some people and some events seem bigger than life, a person can begin to believe that it is only bigger-than-life actions that make a difference. It may seem that one can make more of an impact when a neighbor's house is burning than when it is still standing and he just needs a visit. But that is not so. Good deeds do not need to be show-stopping. There is really no such thing as a *small* good act. Henry Wadsworth Longfellow said it this way: "Give what you have. To someone, it may be better than you dare to think." ("Evangeline.")

Elder Richard L. Evans said, "We can't do everything for everyone everywhere, but we can do something for someone somewhere." (*Richard L. Evans' Quote Book*, Salt Lake City: Publisher's Press, 1971, p. 51.)

It is not the occasional big gesture that makes a good parent, a memorable friend, a warm neighbor. Rather, it is a thousand little things. The parent who knows how to stop in a hurried schedule long enough to take everyone out on the back porch to celebrate the sunset. The friend who can see you at your worst and still believe the best of you. The neighbor who shovels snow from your walk before you get there. None of them are really big acts, but they can change your life and your outlook. Aren't you glad that that parent, that friend, that neighbor didn't believe that what they did wouldn't make any difference?

And how many other people contribute to your life every day whom you never see and never thank? Consider the man who clears the garbage from your street; the person who invented the refrigerator; the man who keeps the power lines working; the artist who painted the picture on your wall. If ever they were tempted to think that what they do does not make any difference, let them stop for a year or let them never have done their work, and see how miserable the world would become.

Richard L. Evans also said, "Nothing does itself—that is nothing constructive. Someone has to do everything. . . . Classes don't teach themselves; food doesn't prepare itself; . . . words don't memorize themselves. Someone has to lay every brick and drive every nail, make everything that is made, do everything that is done, think everything that is thought." (Ibid., p. 47.)

What you do makes a great deal of difference in this world. The important thing is to believe that.

Let me tell you a story about the impact of one person: Ettie Lee. She was a schoolteacher for forty-four years. She was a remarkable teacher, drawing upon a philosophy gained from her father, "Those who draw from the well of life should put something back." During her many years of teaching, she became concerned about the number of bright young boys in her class who got in trouble with the law and were sent to institutions.

"Convinced that institutions only taught young people to become inmates of institutions, Ettie Lee approached child welfare groups, correctional institutions, and the courts to plead the cause of misguided youth, but soon realized that if someone were going to provide homes instead of institutions for these boys, she would have to do it herself. Knowing that her own income wouldn't suffice, she followed the advice in a library book on real estate investments, saved half her salary each month and began to invest.

"Her courage and perception were phenomenal, her methods unorthodox. Over the years she accumulated investment properties which gave her enough income so she could have retired comfortably, but instead she lived frugally in one of her smallest apartments, her needs met by her teacher's pension, and used all her earnings to finance her real life's work—rehabilitating wayward boys. With her savings, she finally had enough to buy a big, comfortable ranch out in the country where troubled boys could go live in a family setting while straightening out their lives." (Booklet produced and distributed by the Ettie Lee Foundation.)

Today the work she started is carried out in many such homes, and over four thousand boys—the hopeless, the delinquent, the incorrigible, the boys abandoned by society and headed for lives of crime and despair—have been through her homes and changed their lives.

What if Ettie Lee had said, "What I do doesn't make any difference"? Were her acts so world-stopping, so big? They seem so to us, but to her it was probably just the result of many small sacrifices and consistent effort. And without her the world would have been a different, a diminished place.

The world is diminished when any of us use that excuse for giving up. What you do makes a great deal of difference to someone. And it makes a great deal of difference to you. In an age when people are searching desperately for happiness, when many finally give up and are content just to avoid pain, your happiness will be directly commensurate with the service you give. Remember, even in your moments of self-doubt, that you were sent here to make a difference.

Ask of God, Who Giveth Liberally

"The class of noisy boys in a German primary school was being punished by their teacher. They were assigned the problem of adding together all the numerals from 1 to 100.

"The boys settled down, scribbling busily on their slates—all but one. This boy looked off into space for a few moments, then wrote something on his slate and turned it in. His was the only right answer.

"When the amazed teacher asked how he did it, the boy replied, 'I thought there might be some short cut, and I found one: 100 plus 1 is 101; 99 plus 2 is 101; 98 plus 3 is 101 and if I continue the series all the way to 51 plus 50, I have 101 50 times which is 5050.'

"After this episode, the young scholar received special tutoring from his teacher. The boy grew up to be Karl Friedrich Gauss, the great mathematician of the 19th century." ("Personal Glimpses," *Reader's Digest*, September 1961, p. 11.)

This story is striking to me because I see in the classroom a parallel to the world where most of us spend a life of desperate hurry trying to accomplish tasks of sometimes questionable worth. Like boys who scribble on their slates adding useless numbers, we often run unsure of our reasons.

No time to think, to ponder, to be sure of where we head or why. The object seems to be speed alone. Can we cross off our bulging lists of things to do before the list is doubled again? But in this story, we note that the one who finished the task was not the one who plunged ahead frantically. No, it was the boy who paused before his task to gather wisdom. He sought direction before he worked.

Why are we so little like him? Why do we confuse speed for direction in life, hurry for insight? Too often we buy products that we are led to believe we need by convincing commercials. We adopt goals because other people seem to value them. Everyone can tell you about the right neighborhood, the right house, the right job. We sometimes give less planning to raising our children than we would to building a storage shed. We may give less effort to keeping up our marriage than keeping up our car. None of this is really because we mean to be careless or stupid. It is just that the world is so much with us, and we waste our energies on misdirected goals and yearnings that do not merit our regard. Like the boys who had to add the numbers 1 to 100, there is so much to do and so little time.

A great and often unused promise in the New Testament says, "If any of you lack wisdom, let him ask of God, that giveth to all men liberally, and upbraideth not; and it shall be given him." (James 1:5.) The Lord has promised to give us what we, as mortals with limited vision, most lack— wisdom, direction, insight. He has promised us that He will give not with stinginess, but liberally. He will help us pick our way through the dilemmas and frustrations that every life is filled with. He will shed light where there seems to be nothing but darkness and confusion. When we are bombarded with the pressures of the world, He can help us understand what has true merit for us. Not to call on Him for wisdom is to be like children lost in a tall forest who refuse to call for direction to the guard standing on a high tower who has the vantage to see it all.

One man tells a story of his very personal quest for wisdom with a business problem. Let me tell it in his own words:

"The pressures of my job as a sales manager for a home building company can be very acute at times. I had been a member of the Church about six months when two problems confronted me one morning, each within about five minutes of the other. First, one of the salesmen rejected an offer to join with the rest of the sales team for a lunch given by the company. I was hurt because we were a close-knit, friendly team.

"As I sat miserably in my office, contemplating the problem, the company manager came in to remind me that we had about a half million dollars worth of new homes that had been unsold for a year. He wanted me to make a positive effort, work miracles if necessary, to get them sold.

"Heavy with the weight of these two problems, I picked up my jacket as soon as he left and walked out to the car. I drove to one of the offending houses, unlocked it, went inside, and locked the door behind me. I walked up the stairs, and in the empty lounge I knelt to pray. At that moment something unusual happened. Before I could even think the words that I had wanted to say to my Heavenly Father, in a beautiful clear light within my closed eyes I seemed to see my problem salesman happily accepting the challenge to sell all those difficult homes; he also agreed not to be permitted to sell easier ones until the others were sold. He would be given a completely free hand to organize his own campaign, promotions, advertising, and his own time. He would be rewarded by a higher rate of commission.

"Within two months those homes that a previous salesman had had so much trouble with were sold by my problem salesman. He was a changed man after his successful response to a big challenge, and the manager was delighted." (Roy B. Webb, "Businessman's Prayer in an Upper Room," *Ensign*, January 1976, pp. 50-51.)

What a difference asking the Lord for wisdom made to this businessman. And it can make a difference to you too. The Lord has asked His followers to ask him for help. Why would they ever hesitate?

If you would draw upon the powers of heaven to give your life new meaning and direction, you must start simply by having faith that the Lord is there and that He cares about you as an individual. You are not just a member of a faceless mob before Him. You can learn this even from observing His mortal ministry. When He met the woman of Samaria at the well, He already knew all about her and told her about her life. He recognized her when He felt the touch of just one hand on His hem in a crowd. And though He fed a multitude with fish and loaves, it was to each individual that He was responding.

This faith about His knowledge of His children teaches you that you can be very specific in your prayers, carrying to the Lord your true feelings and concerns. Too often a person will hurry through his prayers, speaking in broad generalizations, a kind of spiritual shorthand. "Help me in my work," he might say, instead of spelling out specifically what are the problems and challenges he faces there. "Bless the children" rolls easily from the lips, instead of asking for help with one child's problem with self-esteem and another child's need to learn responsibility. Be specific. He is interested, and, unlike most mortals, He will hear you out.

Next, don't believe that any problem you have is too trivial to take before Him. Some have believed that nothing on earth should hurt or bewilder them as long as they know that God is in His universe, and all will be made right and good at the final day. But somehow, even if you know that this frustration is temporary and that that question will fade away, life is difficult all the same. Whatever your problems and questions are, if they are important to you, they are important to the Lord. Christ showed again and again in His mortal ministry intense feeling for human-size fears and griefs. Isn't it fitting that One who joined us in humanity should understand our worries and weaknesses? Knowing that Lazarus would live again, Jesus still wept at his death. He calmed the Sea of Galilee when the apostles were frightened of the storm. And He will calm your troubled waters. Your problem is never trivial to him.

So, if you lack wisdom as you run through life, unsure of why you run, pause and ask of God. He will give liberally.

Give It All You've Got

The crowd was hushed and breathless. Before them a young man was about to compete in one of the most difficult of all athletic competitions. It would take total concentration, great strength, and perfect balance. In the complete coordination of the body and the mind, no sport exceeds gymnastics, and no phase of gymnastics exceeds the flying rings. Every moment must be virtually perfect. Any variation from an uncontrolled muscle can send the suspended body soaring in the wrong direction. The slightest miscalculation can destroy a routine and even break a few bones.

At any level, the flying rings are challenging. At the highest levels, they may well be the epitome of coordination and concentration of body and mind.

Shun Fujimoto was poised at that epitome, in the 1976 Olympics in Montreal. The Japanese gymnastics team had a chance for the gold, but they needed Shun, and he knew it. He also knew better than anyone in the world at that moment what it would cost him to do his part. The cost would be paid in searing pain, but he would not back down.

A murmur went through the sports arena as Shun ascended to the rings. The crowd was incredulous, for from his hip to the tip of his toes, Shun was wearing a cast! After years of training and preparation, he had come to this the greatest moment in an athlete's career, the Olympics, only to break his leg in practice the day before the competition.

There was no way he could compete—but there he was, ready to try. No one, including Shun himself, knew quite how he could compensate for the extra weight and stiffness of the cast, for the crucial lack of mobility of his leg. And perhaps more than any of these handicaps, there was the mental distraction, bordering on torture, of knowing what awaited him in a few short seconds.

But he mounted the rings. He soared, he twisted, and he rotated gracefully. His routine was building to a climax and a close. Then came the moment of truth that only he could fully anticipate. His graceful body flashed through the air in a triple somersault and a full twist; then down his body arched in a perfect landing.

He stood poised and looked up smartly for the final instant of his routine. It was over. Only then did he allow his broken leg and the shattered cast to crumple beneath him. He had done it!

The crowd burst into applause, and the judges posted Shun's score: the most perfect performance and the highest score he had ever achieved in his gymnastics career. The audience went wild.

"It is beyond my comprehension how he could land without collapsing in screams. What a man!" said an Olympics doctor.

"Yes, the pain shot through me like a knife," Shun said. "It brought tears to my eyes. But now I have a gold medal, and the pain is gone." (*Newsweek*, August 2, 1976, p. 61.)

A crucial instant of courage and an eternity of memories. The gold medal, of course, is merely a symbol of what Shun did. But his unconquerable spirit will shine with the memory of what he accomplished.

We all face ultimate moments in our lives, not so dramatic perhaps, but adapted exactly to our needs and strengths. We may not be tested beyond our limits to endure, and we may not be crushed by forces outside ourselves, but we may rest assured that in this life we are and will be tested to the utmost of our abilities.

To some, it may be a sharp and distinct challenge with a shattering explosion of pain at the end, as it was for Shun. For others, it may be a long, drawn-out testing. It may be a trial of faith and patience, as we struggle to become what we were meant to be. Our tests are adapted to our needs, our temperament, our personality, but they are there. How else could we learn what we can really do? How could we feel the greatest thrill this life has to offer, the thrill of accomplishment? Whether the challenge is a matter of life and death, or something less serious, such as standing up to give your first public talk when your legs feel as solid as two strands of spaghetti, there is no satisfaction to match coming through in the clutch.

One of the current buzz words in our society is "burnout." People in various occupations and walks of life are being "burned out," they say, by stresses and demands placed upon them. Now, I would not minimize the problems any of us face in this world. They are very real. But we must learn to deal with them rather than having them deal with us. The real question in the refining fires of this life is whether one will be a burner or a burnee, whether we will be burned out by stresses and circumstances or catch fire ourselves and determine our own destiny.

The people who lived at Corinth in the early days of Christianity were beset by trials and temptations on every side. Some of them felt justified in giving up, but the apostle Paul wrote to them, "God . . . will not suffer you to be tempted above that ye are able; but will with the temptation also make a way to escape, that ye may be able to bear it." (1 Corinthians 10:13.) As the old saying has it, He will temper the wind to the shorn lamb, but there will be wind.

There seems to be a feeling in some circles these days that the best life is one that is free from stresses and strains, floating unbothered in a warm sea of pleasure with no demands made on our body, mind, or spirit, like so many soggy jellyfish. But the distinguishing feature of jellyfish is that they develop no backbone, and neither would we on such a diet for our spirits.

So leap out of bed every morning with a prayer of thanks for the challenges the new day will offer you, thanks unto heaven for the compliment of letting you show your spunk. And when the going gets rough, remember the words of an injured athlete who wouldn't quit: "Now I have a gold medal, and the pain is gone."

Use Your Time Wisely and Well

One of the influential philosophers of our time, in my opinion, is Charles Schultz, whose crowd of wise and witty kids appears in the Peanuts comic strips. One of my favorite cartoons shows Lucy asking Charlie Brown, "What is your favorite day, Charlie Brown?"

Charlie answers, "I'm sort of fond of tomorrow."

And who of us isn't? In a way that's all right. Tomorrow is filled with all sorts of new possibilities, opportunities, and adventure. It's the exciting, somewhat mysterious, intriguing future. Thank goodness for tomorrows when we can improve on our performance of today.

But if we're not careful, instead of an open-handed, hearty, welcoming friend, tomorrow can become the sultry-voiced, seductive thief of our time called procrastination. In fact, procrastination will do more than just steal our valuable time; it will even make our decisions and direct our lives, if we give it a chance. There is a bit of advice handed around by the test pilots of airplanes. They say that in the event something goes wrong with the plane, the pilot will make a decision to bail out or try to bring the plane in. He will make this decision whether he wants to or not, they say, because no decision plus the passage of time equals a decision.

Now that's a pretty profound equation for a pilot watching the fateful numbers of his altimeter whiz by. And it is also the same equation facing each of us in a little less dramatic setting. No decision plus the passage of time equals a decision. Postponement or procrastination of something doesn't do away with the consequences.

Aesop, the ancient Greek fable teller, tried to get that point across in his story of the ant and the grasshopper. The grasshopper didn't deliberately decide to go hungry that winter; he just didn't get around to deciding to do anything about it. The ant decided early in the summer to stock his shelves, and so he had the whole season to get ready for winter.

And thus it is with us. Our lives will spin out before us one day at a time, but what happens in those days will depend in large part on the decisions we make and when we make them.

A friend came to me the other day to ask my advice on whether he should go back to college and get a degree. He was a bit older than the average student, and would have to go at it part-time for a number of years. He wanted the degree, but he was concerned about the time. "By the time I got my degree I'd be forty years old," he told me. I said to him, "That's interesting. How old will you be if you don't get it?"

Most of us are afflicted a little or a lot by that old ailment called put-it-off-itus. We want to do something, but we are forever preparing to get ready to commence to start to begin. President Spencer W. Kimball has two good words of advice on a little sign on his desk. It says simply, "Do it." That's sound counsel. How many good works, how many fine intentions, how many great plans, how many marvelous dreams are waiting around for the dreamer, the planner, the intender to come to terms with those two little profound words and just "do it"?

"But the job is so big, so overwhelming, so intimidating," I hear people say. Sure it is, but you can eat an elephant—if you take it one bite at a time. You don't have to tackle the whole carcass in one sitting; just kid yourself a little and say, "Hey, I'll just begin with a nibble off the old hind leg here."

One of my friends, a writer, uses this technique when he faces that dreaded disease of all pundits and pen pushers called writer's block. That's when your mind turns to mush and a blank piece of paper can look like Mount Everest sitting in front of you. When that happens, he tells himself, "Hey, I'm not going to write *War and Peace* this morning. I'm just going to smudge up this white piece of paper with a few black marks and scrawls, that's all." This helps him get over the inertia of dead rest; then, once he gets his mind in the harness and started down the furrow, it's much more prone to keep plowing, he tells me.

"To every thing there is a season, and a time to every purpose under the heaven," said King Solomon in his famous discourse on the subject. (Ecclesiastes 3:1.) Another problem with procrastination is that it throws our timing off. We find ourselves scrambling to prepare for an opportunity when we should be taking advantage of it.

Not long ago a young teenage girl was walking with her father when he had a heart attack. She saved his life with emergency medical techniques she had learned in school. Now, if she had had to run back home, get her books, and study the lesson she had put off learning, it would have been too late for her father.

"Dost thou love Life?" asked Benjamin Franklin. "Then do not squander Time, for that's the stuff Life is made of." (*Poor Richard's Almanac.*) Old Ben followed his own advice so well that he crammed the careers of five or six people into his eighty-four years. He was, as you know, a statesman, inventor, publisher, author, and philosopher. He knew, as do so many successful people, that time is money, and he said as much in some of his practical aphorisms.

Truly time does behave like that slippery substance. Like money, it can be saved, invested, budgeted, and profitably used. Unfortunately it can also be squandered, wasted, and lost.

When we are young, it is easy to feel we have an unlimited time bank account as the endless days and years stretch out before us. But soon we begin to see that time is perhaps our most precious possession. We don't want to hoard it; rather we want to spend it wisely and well.

In Morocco some years ago a French administrator named Lyaoute learned that cedar trees had once graced the nearby hills, but the trees had been cut down and destroyed through wars and desolation. He ordered them replaced, but one of the local people chided him a bit. "Sir," he said, "Those were ancient cedars. They take two thousand years to grow." But the administrator knew the value of time. He answered, "Then we must plant them at once." It is never too early nor too late to begin a worthy project.

A Change of Prescription

Norman Schachter, a veteran National Football League referee, said that during the halftime of a championship NFL game, the weather was pushing zero, and he and the other officials ran to the dressing room to get warm. As he was relaxing, he received a telegram from his eye doctor, who had prescribed his contact lenses. It read: "Saw the first half on television. It's time for a new prescription." (*Reader's Digest*, December 1974, p. 201.)

Referees aren't the only ones who sometimes don't see clearly. We're all subject to distorted vision, and perhaps there is no place where it happens more frequently than in our search for love.

Most of us spend a great deal of our time trying to get other people interested in us. We want friends, neighbors, and business colleagues to notice the good things we do. We want them to cry when we hurt and to admire our strengths, and we go to great lengths to get their attention. "Notice me," we cry out in a thousand silent ways, like little children who want their mother's attention. "Hey, watch this." But the fact is, it is almost impossible to make people interested in us. They are too interested in themselves to divert their attention.

If you doubt that, just ask yourself, where do your eyes go first when you look at a group photo that you've been a part of?

If we want to be loved, then we have to start by being genuinely interested in others, not by trying to make others interested in us. The secret to human relations is not in trying to be noticed, but in swinging the focus and noticing others, in giving abundantly what every human being on this earth craves—love.

We are all familiar enough with our own feelings to know that laced generously among those times of competence and triumph are times when we feel inadequate and stupid. We know that we are just as likely to have days where everything goes wrong as to have days when we feel like conquering heroes. Behind our bravado and bright faces, our hearts are sometimes bleeding with unspoken cares. Our brows are wrinkled with worries and frustrations more often than we care to admit. And often, just when we think we've adjusted to our life as it is, it throws us a curve. We lose someone we love, or an expectation is dimmed, or our security is shattered, and we have to start over again to feel good about it all.

None of us is alone in these feelings. Though we shine up our appearances for one another, each of us knows his own suffering, left alone in a moment when no one's eyes are watching.

Do you want love to be a part of your life, then? Penetrate this great secret of the human heart and give to others the support and comfort they so badly need.

How many times have you thought, "I wish a friend would do this kind act for me." "I wish my spouse would notice this need." "I wish someone would call just because they liked me." That is the very moment you need to stop and think, "Have I done that kind deed for my friend?" "When

was the last time I noticed that need in my husband or wife?"
"Did I call someone just to say I liked him?"

Our own yearnings are great teachers of what others are
yearning for also. It is rewarding to learn to see the world not
just through our own eyes, but through the eyes of another,
adopting their frame of experience long enough to understand their needs. When we do this, we learn that we aren't
alone, but are marvelously connected to others. The whole
world groans with the same salt tears, laughs the same
laughter.

At the Last Supper, Jesus Christ, who had only minutes
to sum up His life and ministry before He was to leave His
trembling disciples to carry on the work alone, said this: "As
I have loved you, . . . love one another." (John 13:34.)

This was the thrust of His work in a sentence, the legacy
He left for His disciples to pass on.

And only hours later, when He hung on the cross, He
gave us a lesson in what His kind of love was. He was experiencing in every cell of His body the most painful and
barbaric death man had conceived. James E. Talmage
described it thus: "Death by crucifixion was at once the most
lingering and most painful of all forms of execution. The vic-
tim lived in ever increasing torture, generally for many
hours, sometimes for days. The spikes so cruelly driven
through hands and feet penetrated and crushed sensitive
nerves and quivering tendons, yet inflicted no mortal
wound. The welcome relief of death came through the
exhaustion caused by intense and unremitting pain, through
localized inflammation and congestion of organs incident to
the strained and unnatural posture of the body." (*Jesus the
Christ*, Salt Lake City: Deseret Book, 1973, p. 655.) Added to
all of this was the emotional pain of rejection, betrayal, and
humiliation.

I describe this to point out that if ever there were a time

when Christ could have been excused for thinking only of Himself, this would surely have been it. Pain for most of us is much more commanding than love. Pain absorbs us into ourselves until we have no time for others. Gritting our teeth and surviving seems sufficient. But Christ's love was greater than personal pain. Even as He was in the midst of this torture, His first thought was for others. Looking down from the cross, He saw His mother, Mary, grieving and heartbroken, with no one to take care of her after His death. Then He said to John, His disciple, "Behold thy mother," and from that time on John took Mary into his own home. (John 19:27.) Through His anguish, Christ comforted the thief next to Him and forgave those who reveled at His feet.

Loving as Christ has asked us to love demands that we look out beyond our own problems and needs of the moment to see others—not in terms of what we need, but in terms of what they need. As Dale Carnegie once said, he liked strawberries and cream, but when he went fishing, he tried to think in terms of what the fish liked, and he put worms on the hook.

Too many of us think that we will give of our love and service to others when it is a more convenient time in our lives. When our pressures have subsided, when our frustrations have eased, when we feel full and ready to give, then we will love others and be interested in them. Until then, however, we'd surely like their love and concern to help us along. It just doesn't work that way.

If we want our pressures to subside and our frustrations to ease, we need to quit thinking about them and about ourselves and concentrate on others. We cannot wait for a convenient time to send our bouquets into the world; we have to pick the flowers when they bloom. We must give help when it is needed, not some other time when it fits into our schedule.

On Supreme Court Justice Hugo L. Black's eighty-third birthday, his colleague, frequent opponent, and good friend, John Marshall Harlan, sent him a birthday letter. This is a simple gesture for most men, but Justice Harlan was almost totally blind. To sign an opinion, he found it necessary to turn on a massive set of lights that had been installed above his desk and use a large, single-lens magnifying glass. With the glass on his eye actually touching the paper, he would struggle painfully to complete his signature. It was the only writing he did.

The birthday note to Justice Black covered a page. When he read it, he folded it and put it carefully in his pocket, then turned his back on his clerk for a few minutes. When he turned around, his eyes were full of tears. "He wrote it himself." he said. (*Reader's Digest*, January 1977, p. 131.)

Justice Harlan had every excuse possible for forgetting Justice Black's birthday. But, despite his infirmity, he sent his birthday card.

May we have the wisdom not to seek for the attention of others, but to give attention to all the souls who hunger as we so often do.

Putting Pain
in Perspective

The Roanoke, Virginia, *Times and World News* reported a few years ago that Thomas G. Nye, a full-time professor and head of the biology department at a fine university, was out turkey hunting at dawn one weekend and drew a bead on a flock of what he thought were turkeys in a tree. Instead, he brought down two prime buzzards, protected species in his state. His only consolation, he said, as he took a ribbing from fellow faculty members, was that his biological specialty is botany, not zoology.

The wisdom of even the best of us can sometimes fail. And nowhere is this more evident than in our attitude toward pain. It is the nature not only of human beings, but of all living things, to shrink from pain and avoid it at any cost. Just as white rats retreat from electrical shocks, so human beings use any escape mechanism to withdraw from personal suffering.

We would, given our own hand at things, fashion a world without torment and disappointment. As Charlie Brown's friend Lucy said of life's ups and downs, "Why can't I just move from one 'up' to another 'up'? Why can't I just go from an 'up' to an 'upper-up'?" We're with you, Lucy.

But in the course of every life, there *is* pain and opposition. Lucy may speak for us today, but Augustine's words ring across the centuries: "God had one Son on earth without sin, but never one without suffering."

It is the universal condition of mortal men to have bodies that are subject to disease and cold and want, bodies that die, leaving survivors behind stricken with sorrow. And it is the particular condition of each individual heart to have sorrows customized for it, when status or self-esteem is lost, hard work is not rewarded, or youthful dreams remain unrealized. To be human is to know times when the thorn is in our flesh.

This brings us to the inescapable question that has crossed every human mind. Why? Why me? Why now? Why should I, who want nothing more than to live out a happy, undisturbed life, have to face pain and opposition? Even the most faithful person may feel that the Lord has forsaken him when the fire burns particularly hot. "Enough," he seems to say. "I've had enough."

In the midst of trial, we may wonder why the Lord allows it to continue. Like a patient crying out for anesthesia, we cry out for our tribulations to be removed, and often they continue.

We are like the child who, upon hearing "The Three Bears," changed the story. When Goldilocks ate the porridge, it was all right, because her mother just dished out some more. And when Goldilocks broke the chair, her father fixed it right then. She didn't want any hardship in her story. And we don't want any hardship in our lives. "Remove it," we plead. "Remove it now."

Of the various tragedies around us, President Spencer W. Kimball has said, "Could the Lord have prevented these tragedies? The answer is, Yes. The Lord is omnipotent, with all power to control our lives, save us pain, prevent all accidents, drive all planes and cars, feed us, protect us, save us from labor, effort, sickness, even from death, if he will. But he will not.

"We should be able to understand this, because we can realize how unwise it would be for us to shield our children from all effort, from disappointments, temptations, sorrows, and suffering. . . .

"If we looked at mortality as the whole of existence, then pain, sorrow, failure, and short life would be a calamity. But if we look upon life as an eternal thing stretching far into the pre-earth past and on into the eternal post-death future, then all happenings may be put in proper perspective." (*Tragedy or Destiny*, Salt Lake City: Deseret Book, 1977, p. 2.)

Maybe what we need to get us through life, then, is not the prevention of pain, but a perspective on it. If the Lord, who could make cold days warm and hungry stomachs full, does not do so, we can be sure there is a reason, one that springs not out of his indifference, but his love.

Just as a violin makes music only when it is stretched, and a kite can rise only against the wind, so the soul of man expands under the pressure of pain. Only when we have run straight up against the limits of our frailty do we learn what it is to depend upon the Lord. Sorrow seems to open up an intensity in our heavenward yearnings that happiness cannot. Only when we have been sent to the extremities of endurance can we begin to look with real compassion at the plight of others. Otherwise it is easy to believe they deserve their bad breaks. Ironically, the death of our highest hopes may make way for a better dream.

C. S. Lewis put it this way: "Imagine yourself as a living house. God comes in to rebuild that house. At first, perhaps, you can understand what He is doing. He is getting the drains right and stopping the leaks in the roof and so on: you knew that those jobs needed doing and so you are not surprised. But presently, He starts knocking the house about in a way that hurts abominably and does not seem to make sense. What on earth is He up to? The explanation is that He is building quite a different house from the one you thought of—throwing out a new wing here, putting on an extra floor there, running up towers, making courtyards. You thought you were going to be made into a decent little cottage: but He is building a palace." (*Mere Christianity*, New York: Macmillan, 1960, p. 174.)

What remains, then, while we face the pain of being remodeled is the choice of how we will respond to it all. We can let bitter days embitter us or we can understand, as Victor Frankl said of living in a concentration camp, that "the one freedom that conditions cannot take from us is our freedom to form a healthy attitude toward those very conditions, grim as those may sometimes be." (Neal A. Maxwell, *All These Things Shall Give Thee Experience*, Salt Lake City: Deseret Book, 1979, p. 40.)

While we may not have the power to choose absolutely whether we will know health or wealth, sorrow or loneliness, we do have the power to choose who we will be in the face of it. Will pain teach us patience or irritability? Will affliction make us turn against the Lord or toward Him? Will we have the faith to face a world where every trace of the Lord seems to have disappeared and still call on Him?

"O my Father, if it be possible, let this cup pass from me," prayed Jesus in the Garden of Gethsemane, "nevertheless not as I will, but as thou wilt." (Matthew 26:39.) Christ knows the anguish of wanting a trial to disappear. And more important, he teaches us how to endure when it doesn't. He was not broken. He never turned on His Father. He didn't forsake the world.

Malcolm Muggeridge wrote, "The essential feature, and necessity of life, is to know reality, which means knowing

God. Otherwise our mortal existence is, as Saint Teresa of Avila said, 'no more than a night in a second-class hotel.'" ("The Great Liberal Death Wish," *Imprimis*, May 1979.) If, in order to know the Lord—the ultimate reality of existence—it is necessary to pass through pain, so be it. It is a small price for this dearest of all privileges. May we have the power to endure, and to endure beautifully.

Who's to Decide
for You?

Life offers us a million choices. Have you ever stopped to think about it? Heinz used to have only 57 varieties; now they have over 2,000. More than 30,000 books are published every year in America. Which are you going to read? You can choose to have your toothpaste either plain white or striped, and you may have a television set that beams more than twenty stations to you. How can you decide?

Most of us can handle these small decisions in life. They don't really trouble us. But not all of life's decisions are so trifling. Almost from your first breath, you've been making your destiny by what you choose, carving out your very life. What will you do for a living? Which school will you attend? Whom will you marry? Where will you live? And finally, and most important, who will you be?

These decisions aren't insignificant or trifling. And because they aren't, many people may find themselves trembling before them, nervous every day to see how it will all work out, looking at the future with worry and insecurity. They want some guarantee that every important decision will be the right one. They want a seal of approval stamped on tomorrow.

Since, however, guarantees are hard to come by and

seals are not solid, we may find ourselves looking around to
see what others decide and going with the drift. We poll the
majority and hope the best decision wins. We keep an eye
over our shoulder to see what others are doing. It's easy to be
puppets dancing when someone else moves the string, easy
to compromise ourselves before the pressure of popularity or
expediency. Oh, there are dangers in such a strategy.

Kieth Merrill, a filmmaker who has won an Academy
Award, tells this story from his youth:

"When I was a young man I lived in a small community
close to the mountains. I was a lifeguard and did lots of
swimming. . . . We went swimming at a place called East
Canyon, a beautiful man-made reservoir. The dam is in a
narrow neck of the canyon between sheer rock walls.

"None of us had boats, so we couldn't water ski, but we
would do what we called cliff diving. We'd climb up those
rocks and dive into the reservoir. We'd always wear tennis
shoes because the rocks were so sharp. . . .

"After we'd been there several times and pretty well
knew the rocks, cliffs, and the water depth, two or three of us
hard-core East Canyon divers got into the inevitable teenage
contest of raw courage. One guy climbed up to where they
always dove from and yelled down, 'Hey! I'll bet I dare dive
higher than anybody here!'

"'Ah, go on!'

"So he climbed up to the top of the dam. The dam was
about 50 feet off the water. Diving into the air he arched into
the water, and like a bunch of sheep we crawled up the
rocks, out onto the dam, and all of us dove off. . . .

"Well, that didn't satisfy my friend, and so he said, 'All
right, I'll do one better!' He climbed 60 feet up the side of the
cliff. And not wanting to be outdone, I climbed up by him.
After all, everyone was looking at me. I had a great suntan,
and I was sure everyone expected me to do what he was

doing. He swallowed hard, buried his fear, and from trembling knees arched his back and floated through 60 feet of air into the water.

"I was grateful nobody was watching me as I prepared for my dive. When he cleared and seemed to be all right, I took courage, and I made my dive. By now the other members of our diving contest had backed down, figuring it was a little high. But not my friend. He climbed on up to about 70 feet and once more prepared to dive. From below I could barely see him. Seventy feet is a very long way up on the rocks. I said to myself, 'I hope he doesn't do it because if *he* does it, then obviously *I've* got to do it, and I really don't want to.' About then I saw a pink body float through the air and splash into the water not far from me. He came up laughing, rubbing his shoulders and his eyes, and said, 'Well, Merrill, are you going to do it?'

"'Of course, I'm going to do it!' Everybody on the shore said, 'Yeah, of course he's going to do it!'

"And so I swam back to the shore and climbed up the rocks. I knew I only had the courage for one more jump. . . . I scrambled up 80 feet to the very top of the cliff. As I turned around and looked down, I saw that the cliffs were back away from the water at that height. I had two challenges: to fall 80 feet and to get enough clearance to avoid hitting the rocks at the bottom. Everybody was egging me on in a negative way. 'You're chicken, you're chicken!'

"I stood there all alone, everybody waiting down below. The water was so far away it looked like crinkled tinfoil in the sun. I was just terrified. I was committed, but I had not even based my decision on what I wanted to do or what I felt was right. I had based it on about a half dozen guys whose names I don't even remember who were yelling, 'Hey, chicken, are you going to do it?'

"I realized that in order to make the jump I would have

to run a distance to get enough momentum to carry me over the rocks below. So I backed up and ran as hard as I could toward the edge. I found the mark I had carefully laid at the edge of the rock and sprang out into space. I don't know how long it takes to fall 80 feet, but for me it took about a week. On the way down I remembered distinctly how my parents and teachers had taught me to be careful when making decisions because I could kill myself with a wrong one. I said to myself, 'You have done it; you have killed yourself, because when you hit the water you'll be going so fast that it might as well be concrete.' And when I hit the water I was sure it was concrete. I don't know how far down you go when you jump from 80 feet, but I'll tell you I was a grateful lad when my head finally popped above water. I took a quick inventory to make sure that the throbbing pain in my right thigh didn't designate the loss of anything important." (Kieth Merrill, "Deciding about Decisions," *New Era*, June 1976, p. 12.)

Why did Kieth jump? Did those other guys really care if he did it or not? Are they still somewhere talking about good old Kieth Merrill, who jumped off an eighty-foot cliff? Of course not. But for Kieth it could have been a fatal decision. In that moment, staring off of an eighty-foot cliff, he learned a lesson that he never forgot: You can't trust life's important decisions to somebody else. You can't worry what somebody else will think about you. You have to be certain that your decisions emanate from your own soul, your own convictions, and not from the whims of others.

Yet many people are prone to that mistake. A friend gets a new house or a prestigious job, and suddenly you are miserable thinking you need a new house or a better job. You hear that everyone is seeing this movie or laughing at that joke, and suddenly you think this movie or that joke is appropriate.

But after the crowd has vanished and the laughter has

ebbed, you are left alone, responsible for your own life. You are accountable for living up to your best convictions, making your own decisions. They will never be as important to anyone else as they are to you.

So when the voices of the world crowd in upon you, step aside to decide, and then verify your plans with the only voice you can always trust, your Heavenly Father.

It's All in How
You See It

A New England mountain called the Great Stoneface appears to be a perfect profile if viewed from a certain vantage. The features are clear and majestic. But just move one hundred yards, and suddenly the Great Stoneface is nothing but a piece of slate that is sluffing off the mountain.

It's all in how you see it.

The Windmill, a charming inn on Lake Winnipesaukee in New Hampshire, has a unique message on the sack guests use to take home leftover food. Most restaurants refer to these sacks as doggie bags, food fit only for Fido, so if you want to eat it when you get home, you feel half guilty. But the Windmill calls these sacks "The Rest of the Best."

It's just another case in which it's all in how you see it. Life, in fact, is just a great exercise in which the eyes have it, the eyes with which we see.

Have you ever really stopped to think that your feelings about life, about the people around you, are only what you make them? One of life's basic facts is that you can make your attitude about anything whatever you want it to be. You're in control, and you decide every morning if you're going to be happy. You decide with every new meeting what you see in others.

Most of us don't think about that very often. In fact, it's very common to hear expressions such as "He makes me so mad," "She makes me sick." People who make that kind of statement are just fooling themselves. He can't make you mad and she can't make you sick. Nobody can make you anything. You make yourself mad, happy, or patient. How can anyone else choose your feelings for you?

It is certainly true that disappointing and frustrating things happen around you all the time. Life is full of thorns. They alone, though, can't upset you. You choose your reaction to them.

You would probably laugh at the teenager who drove into the side of the garage and then got out of his car and kicked the garage. The garage was hardly at fault; it hadn't moved. But it's just as silly to blame something outside yourself for how you feel.

When you really stop to think about it, it's an awesome power to be able to determine your own thoughts, to be able to simply decide if you like yourself and your life, but it is the power the Lord has given you. You're in charge of your own attitude, a trust given especially to you. It wasn't given to your parents, or your mate, or your neighbor, or even your environment, which always takes a lot of unwarranted blame for how we feel. It's how *you* choose to see and think about things that determines your whole feeling about life.

Think, for example, about the drive you take every morning to work or to school. If you want to think of it as a boring slab of time, a long, gray expanse stretching out before you as you head for something you dread, that's just what it will be. But if you choose to think of it as an early-morning adventure with the world just waking up, the sunlight playing off the trees, another day and another great challenge, then that's just what it will be. It's up to you.

And you are the one who will determine your own success in the world by how you think of yourself. Everyone has failed at one thing or another. We've all been the object of somebody else's criticism or unkind remarks. We all know more intimately than anyone else our weaknesses, our physical imperfections. There's a whole world out there of people walking around thinking their noses are too big or their eyes are too small, people everywhere remembering, long after they have passed, the times they felt stupid and tongue-tied, the times they were late when they wanted to be on time, angry when they wanted to be calm.

Just as you can determine your attitude about the world around you, you can determine your attitude toward yourself. Any unfriendliness or criticism has no power to affect you unless you take it into your consciousness. You do not need to dwell on past errors or physical imperfections. You can choose your own reaction, your own thoughts.

I once knew a young man who had been reared on a pig farm, and frankly, he was much more comfortable with the pigs than with people, with whom he felt shy and withdrawn. The day he left the farm to register for high school, he passed a playing field where some boys were tossing a football. It looked great, so he decided to sign up to play. The problem, though, was that he didn't have any football shoes or the money to buy them. Then he remembered that his older cousin had been a football star at the same school. He visited his cousin and asked whether he could borrow his shoes. His cousin gave him the shoes but warned, "Don't you disgrace them."

The young man made the team as a defensive tackle. In the first game of the season, he found himself at the first line of scrimmage, hunkered down opposite a big, mean-looking senior lineman. He took one look at the fearsome opponent, gulped, and said to himself, "I can't knock him down. But my cousin could—and I'm wearing my cousin's shoes." So he went ahead and knocked him down, and kept on knocking him down all through the game.

Did his cousin's shoes really make any difference in this young man's playing ability? Did they give him more strength or coordination? Of course not. He had the ability, the strength, and the coordination all along. The shoes just helped him believe.

I once saw a magazine advertisement that displayed a picture of a bumblebee. Under the picture was the caption "The bumblebee can't fly. By all the laws of aerodynamics, its body is too bulky for its wings, but the bumblebee doesn't know it, so it flies." Marcus Aurelius put it this way, "Our life is what our thoughts make it."

Why is it, then, that we ever let someone else or something else choose our attitudes? It is probably because we forget who's in control. We forget that of all the precious gifts the Lord has given us, surely the most precious is the chance to choose for ourselves our direction, our dreams, and, most of all, our attitudes.

When you look in the mirror, is it your smile or your wrinkles that you observe? When you pass a puddle on the street, is it the mud at the bottom or the sky it reflects that you are apt to notice? The eyes have it, because it's all in how you see it.

How to Find Yourself

I have a friend who is a person such as you may know, because there are millions throughout the world like her. So far as I know she's never had her name in the newspaper. She's never held a public office or been singled out for public applause. Life has been a bit tough for her because of brain damage she suffered as a child. She gets along all right. She lives in a little house, holds down a daily job, pays her taxes, and tends her flowers, but if ever there were a candidate for anonymity, an example of an unknown and supposedly unimportant person, it is she.

But before you jump to any hasty conclusions, take a little closer look at her life. On a wall in her kitchen is a carefully marked calendar. All the birthdays of just about everybody she knows are carefully circled on that calendar, and none of them has a birthday without a card and a note from her. For many of her friends, that is the only recognition they get that they have been born. But she always remembers.

And it isn't just birthdays. Down the street two blocks is an old man who lives alone with only his cat for company. Last Thanksgiving Day he heard a knock at the door. There stood my friend with a TV dinner she had purchased for his Thanksgiving Day feast. Now others in their most thoughtful and generous moments might have remembered that man on a Thanksgiving Day. Some might have got themselves together and actually taken him something or invited him in. But I submit that almost none would have had the thoughtfulness of my friend.

As she handed the old man the TV dinner, she smiled and held out in the other hand a can of cat food. Yes, some who fancy themselves caring people would have remembered the old man, but how many would have remembered his cat?

My quiet friend has made a life-style of these little acts. She is working her way toward the definition of life that Bernard Berenson gave us. He said, "A complete life may be one ending in so full an identification with the not-self that there is no self left to die." Is she unimportant? Not to the people whose lives she touches. Is she well paid? Not in money, and not in fame or glory. She'll probably never be a celebrity, but then what is a celebrity? Fred Allen said, "A celebrity is a person who works hard all his life to become well known, then wears dark glasses to keep from being recognized."

I think about my quiet, obscure friend often when I see beautiful and talented people sitting on their gifts, hoarding their talents for fear they will not be adequately paid or praised for their efforts.

I think about this diligent little doer of good deeds at other times too. I think about her when I hear people lament their loss of self-identification and bemoan and belittle their place in the universe. Now I admit that sometimes those big numbers that the astronomers throw around can make you feel pretty small. But the next time you hear the theories about billions of galaxies, quadrillions of light years, and infinite space, just pull back a minute. Remember that the magnificent thing about this universe of ours is not just its size, but also its order. Nothing is expendable. Everything is important. You are invaluable.

As someone inscribed in Old St. Paul's Church in Baltimore back in 1692, "You are a child of the universe, no less than the trees and the stars; you have a right to be here. And whether or not it is clear to you, no doubt the universe is unfolding as it should."

I hope you are unfolding as you should, unfolding and blossoming to the fullest potential of what you can be. And how do you do that? Albert Einstein said, "The true value of a human being is determined primarily by the measure of the sense by which he has attained liberation from the self." Liberation from the self! That means concentrating on the needs of others, looking out for number two and number three and four, and not getting all worked up about how number one is doing. Don't worry about being successful. Worry about being useful.

Dimitri Mitropoulos, a talented composer and conductor whose musical scores graced the sound tracks of some of America's best-known motion pictures, said it this way; "Success can corrupt: usefulness can only exalt." So be useful, and you'll be appreciated.

As you go about your business in this busy world, stop a moment every now and then and take stock of where you stand. What kind of person have you become? What will you become if you continue in your present direction? Jesus gave us the secret to a successful, happy, and meaningful life when he said, "He that findeth his life shall lose it: and he that loseth his life for my sake shall find it." (Matthew 10:39.)

So go out today, find yourself, and lose your fears, failures, and frustrations as you serve the needs of other people.

The Secret of Columbus's Power

Fall is that time when leaves turn gold, apples are gathered in bushels—and all America turns on the television set to watch football. If you want to know how to tell the teams that will really be successful, then watch for those that *run* onto the field. The players who stick out their chests and charge onto the field as if they mean it are the ones to cheer for. They're the ones who have conviction, and in this world, conviction may be the most important ingredient for success.

But if you really want to learn about conviction, turn to another institution of fall, Christopher Columbus. If *he* had been born in this century and had played football, there'd be no question he'd run onto the field. He'd be a champion. But as it was, he was born into fifteenth-century Genoa, a sandy-haired boy whose blue eyes gazed longingly at the sea.

As a young man, Columbus was eager for adventure; he believed even from his youth that he had a high mission to fulfill. In the words of his eminent biographer, Samuel Eliot Morison, he sailed to America with "a maximum of faith and a minimum of technique, a bare sufficiency of equipment and a super abundance of stout-heartedness." (*Admiral of the Ocean Sea*, Boston: Little, Brown and Co., 1942,

109

pp. 5-6.) He rushed into an unknown sea at seven knots an hour, brimming with confidence that few else had in him. His achievement seems all the more remarkable when it is realized that in 1492 most men in western Europe felt gloomy about the future. Christian civilization seemed to be shrinking in size under the onslaughts of the infidels; there had been no new advance in science for a century, and even the best people were growing cynical and unhappy. What a time to discover a new world!

Where did Columbus find the conviction that his dream was worth pursuing against such gray realities? Where does anyone find the power to meet denial with faith, to believe in himself against tremendous odds? That's the question many people ask themselves in a world that constantly bruises them. And those who answer it successfully have lives charged with energy and power and dreams that come true, while the rest muddle about.

Let's look at Columbus' life at age thirty for some answers. At that age he was well-established. He had arrived, according to the standards of the day. He could have curled up like a cat before a fire, content to sit the rest of his life. But comfort was not his aim in life, as it is never the aim of great men and women. Instead he was captured by an idea bigger than himself: to find another route to the Indies and enlarge the shrinking Christian world. This was no superficial belief, no cover-up for gold-seeking. From his earliest years he'd felt the Spirit of the Lord stirring in his life and wanted nothing greater than to serve Him. He never lost the perspective of what he wanted to do and why. History records that on one voyage, the *Nina* was boarded by a boatful of boisterous natives. It was a time of tumult and shouting, but Columbus didn't hear a thing, for he was praying. He was surprised to learn of the excitement later.

His biographer, Morison, notes that "there can be no

doubt that the faith of Columbus was genuine and sincere, and that his frequent communion with forces unseen was a vital element in his achievement. It gave him confidence in his destiny. . . . This conviction that God destined him to be an instrument for spreading the faith was . . . potent." (Ibid., p. 47.)

Columbus must have felt encouragement from the Lord, because he certainly didn't get much elsewhere. Sponsorship of his voyage was first rejected in Portugal. His brother tried to get sponsorship in England and France; he also was rejected. It took a special committee in Spain six years to even deliberate on the issue. They thought Christopher's mathematics were faulty, his sources poor. When he was finally summoned to meet Queen Isabella, she sent him money for new clothes, an indication of his financial distress. Again he was rejected. In fact, he was several miles out of the city when Isabella sent a special messenger to bring him back. After years of haunting the castles of Europe and being rejected and labeled fool by the most scholarly of committees, he had his sponsor.

A lesser man might have quit amidst this poverty and rejection. But Christopher Columbus had conviction. He started his journey with a prayer, and prayer was part of the daily routine of the ship. In those days before technology gave man false confidence, the sailor was a pious man, and no one more so than Columbus. As the Psalm says, "They that go down to the sea in ships, that do business in great waters; these see the works of the Lord, and his wonders in the deep." (Psalm 107:23-24.)

The voyage started out well enough, but as the days stretched into weeks, the crew began to get restive, uneasy. They had never experienced so many days without seeing land. Who was this foreigner who was leading them into uncharted waters? Who would really care if they threw him overboard? Who knew what lay at the end of their journey—death, starvation, contrary winds that would never take them back to Spain?

The rebellion reached mutinous heights on October 10. But Columbus stayed serene. Scholars agree that his confidence came from an inward assurance in God, not from superior knowledge. He simply told his crew to give him three more days. If they did not spot land by then, he would turn back. He gave no signs that he was even really worried. Finally, on October 12, as the ship scudded over the water, the men caught sight of an island jutting out of a blue sea. When Columbus finally stepped on the new land, he fell to his knees, embraced the ground with his tears, and thanked God for the discovery. He had won the ancient and always recurring battle between belief and doubt. Something had led him on, and he couldn't deny its power.

Goethe once said that every man has only enough strength to complete those assignments that he is fully convinced are important, and in Columbus is an example of a man fully convinced. But the more personal questions each person must ask are: "How can I become fully convinced? In a world that presents me so many choices, in a life where I am unsure of my talents or my worth, how can I have any confidence in my decisions? Life seems to spread before me like an uncharted sea. How can I avoid the 'high waves' and 'mutinous crews'? How can I find the favorable winds?"

Columbus with his ship plunging farther and farther from the known world sets the example. You have as much right as he to call on the ultimate source of inspiration. The Lord didn't stop caring about His children when Columbus reached the New World. He cares about them still, and He is eager to help them chart their courses if they will let him.

No one's life needs to be aimless, to be trial and error, punctuated by false starts and unhappy decisions. If you try to make life a do-it-yourself experience, you will always be running up against your own limitations, your inability to see beyond the horizon.

Call on the Lord. He has asked His children not to place more obligations on their lives, but to change them. He wants you, like Columbus, to discover your high missions. He wants you to feel the power of conviction about your decisions. It's that power that will let you plunge into your private sea with great serenity and conviction.

Where Are the Heroes?

In 1927 a small single engine plane droned toward the coast of France and landed with fuel tanks almost empty. Out stumbled a bleary-eyed but happy young man. The crowd went wild and so did the world. For the young man had pitted his stamina, his courage, and his faith against the trackless Atlantic ocean and won. The world was never the same size after the flight of the "Lone Eagle," Charles Lindbergh.

At the same time in a quieter scene, in the jungles of Africa, another world-shaker worked. This man was a genius in several fields. He could have sat back and enjoyed the plaudits of the crowd as a concert organist or the prestige of the intellectual world as a philosopher and theologian, but he quietly secluded himself in the jungle to serve as a medical doctor to those who needed him most but could pay him least. The human family has been more proud of itself because of Albert Schweitzer.

Dr. Schweitzer's jungle was quiet, but even quieter was the solitude in the mind of a woman who took on the incredible task of trying to learn and reach out to others when she had virtually no way of doing so. Though she was blind, deaf, and dumb, her inconquerable spirit overcame them all, and none of us is quite the same because Helen Keller lived.

This is the quality of heroes who have helped to give us the world we enjoy. Thomas Carlyle wrote, "No great man lives in vain. The history of the world is but the biography of great men."

But where are they today, these great spirits who reach for the stars, who stand on higher ground and lift us up to them? Surely they are among us still, and yet we have not heard from them. The *World Almanac* did a nationwide survey of junior high school students recently and asked them who were the thirty most important and influential people of our day. To these students, the overwhelming majority of heroes were entertainers, principally comedians, with a scattering of sports figures sprinkled in.

Now I certainly have nothing against comedians, humorists, entertainers, and athletes. They have given me some of my most pleasurable hours, but to single them out exclusively as representing the finest efforts that humanity can produce indicates we have a rather shallow view of what life is all about.

The struggle for survival is even more significant than the struggle to move an inflated pigskin over a goal line, even if the occasion is the Super Bowl. Entertainment, sports, the arts, recreation, yes, these are all valuable to the well-balanced life. They may give us clues, insights, and inspiration to go forth and live our own lives more sensitively, more courageously. But they are not life in and of themselves, and when we choose them as the sole representatives of the best we can do, I get an uneasy feeling that we are afraid or unable to see the full scope of our purpose here on earth.

I can't help but remember the fading days of the Roman Empire, when the people lived on a steady diet of bread and circuses. As long as they had food in their stomachs and entertainment to while away their time, they did not have to look out to the wilderness, where the barbarians were gathering in the darkness, sharpening their weapons. And when the darkness closed in around the Romans, they went down, because they had lost the light within themselves.

And so I am asking for a new generation of heroes for us. I am asking those who direct the public spotlight to open up a wider beam and show us a more complete picture of the real world we live in, to use their talents and their creativity to sing the song of the unsung heroes of our day. I mean not just the current scoring leader and the newest comedian, but those whose work and inspiration will live long after the cheers or the laughter have died away. The builders, the planners, yes, and the plodders, the peacemakers, the honest, the caring, thousands of them who would make fascinating fare for the public media if they were properly presented.

But more than that, I am asking for you and me to be heroes. It is out of the best efforts of each of us that some will arise to inspire all of us. We need national and international heroes, yes, but we also need small-town, community, church, and family heroes. Each of us needs people we can relate to, identify with, model our lives after.

Walter MacPeek wrote, "Boys need lots of heroes like Lincoln and Washington. But they also need to have some heroes close by. They need to know some man of towering strength and basic integrity, personally. They need to meet them on the street, to hike and camp with them, to see them in close-to-home, everyday, down-to-earth situations; to feel close enough to them to ask questions and to talk things over man-to-man with them." (Quoted in Spencer W. Kimball, "Boys Need Heroes Close By," *Ensign*, May 1976, p. 47.) The same, of course, goes for young women. We all need heroes.

What does it take to be a hero? An important position? A

cheering crowd? Money? Power? No! It just takes rising to the occasion and giving it the best you've got.

Remember the story of the boy who took a lunch to his older brothers who were fighting in the battle. They told him to go home; he was just in the way. But he saw the chance to give it his best shot, and he did. Nobody expected anything but a minor tragedy as he started down the hill with no armor, no shield, no sword, only his shepherd's bag, his sling, five smooth stones, and, most important, an unshakable faith that the Lord would not let him down. And that day the hills surrounding the valley of Elah rang with the shouts of an inspired Israel as they saw the impossible become the real, and their hero David slay Goliath with his sling and a stone. (1 Samuel 17.)

So go forth and find out what you can do. Do your very best at it, and realize that there is always someone—a little brother or sister, a classmate, a fellow worker, or even a person you pass on the street—who is looking to you for inspiration.

Be a hero!

The Pioneer
in Each Person

An old and very tired man sat and stared into the dying embers of his campfire. In a thin, weak, but resolute voice he began to sing.

> *Come, come, ye Saints, no toil nor labor fear;*
> *But with joy went your way . . .*

There were precious few outward signs of joy among his fellow travelers in that pioneer camp in 1855. They were locked in the grip of an early winter, after having pulled their handcarts through the snow all day. Their scant food supply was almost exhausted, and so was their strength. Huddled against the storm, they tried to catch a few hours' rest before pushing on again in the morning.

In this solemn setting, the old man poured his heart into his quiet song. It was the custom in these "Camps of Israel," as they were called, that if one began this familiar song, "Come, Come, Ye Saints," the whole camp joined in.

But this time, no one did. Rather they listened intently as his voice was wafted away on the mountain wind. He sang:

And should we die before our journey's through,
Happy day! all is well!
We then are free from toil and sorrow, too;
With the just we shall dwell!
But if our lives are spared again
To see the Saints their rest obtain,
O how we'll make this chorus swell—
All is well! all is well!

The old man finished his song and went to bed in his tent. In the morning when his companions came for him, he, like so many others, had passed on to his reward. "Free from toil and sorrow, too," he was now dwelling with the just. All was well with him.

In his story and his song are two lessons we should learn from these noble pioneers. His song was a call to come, to join and band together, to cooperate and help, to share mutual strength. And this they did, those pioneers who struggled across a continent to populate a hostile land that no one else wanted. Only together with mutual care and concern, sympathy and sharing could they have ever withstood the harsh elements, the hostile Indians, and the pressures from those who had driven them from their homes and who would try to drive them out again. They learned to live and give of the best they had. By so doing they not only survived, they prospered. They made the desert blossom as a rose, and they bequeathed this beautiful blossom to those who came later.

Yes, this pioneer song, "Come, Come, Ye Saints," is a rally cry for us today. Come, come let us work, share, live, and forgive each other. Let us bind up the wounds of hatred and overcome the creeds and philosophies that divide us as peoples of the world. Let us overcome the prejudice, the hatred, and the war that make our planet a purgatory instead of a paradise. Let us work together for a better world.

The inspirational song the pioneers sang as they trudged those weary miles has since been sung by tens of thousands and by mighty choirs. It has been broadcast from orbiting satellites and beamed across the face of the world. It is a great rallying call and anthem that will bless all of humankind if we respond to its message, and we must. We must learn to live together, or we shall perish apart.

This is the message of the song, but there is a great meaning also in the solitary singer by the fireside. He himself is a symbol we should study. Quiet, aged, enfeebled, alone in his thoughts, he makes no mighty music with his tired voice, and yet he sings a powerful sermon. He is a pioneer. And by definition a pioneer is one who breaks new ground; who blazes his own trail; who moves and motivates himself and thereby lights the way and smooths the path of those who follow him.

He may never have read these words of Cicero, but they describe him well. The Roman orator wrote: "The altogether courageous and great spirit has, above all, two characteristics. First he . . . is convinced that nothing but moral goodness and propriety are worth admiring and striving for. . . . His second characteristic is that when his soul has been disciplined in this way, he [does] things that are not only great and highly useful, but also deeds that are arduous, laborious and fraught with danger."

This was the spirit of each of these pioneers who came in the days of the old West, the spirit of more than 70,000 who made their individual decisions to leave the comforts of civilization and worldly possessions, friends and loved ones, for a new life where they would be free to worship God according to the dictates of conscience.

It was the spirit of the more than 6,000 who came as far as they could, then died and were left in shallow graves because their loved ones could do no better for them. Each of them was a pioneer with the rugged individualism required to survive in those days. Though they came by the thousands, theirs was not a mass movement, but a collection of individual commitments. Each heart beat to the cadence of its own drummer and throbbed out its own commitment to the cause. Left alone, they would still have made their way west.

That, I believe, is the secret of the success of this generation of giants who fought back the frontier, won over the wilderness and gave us this comfortable world. They were individual pioneers pulling together.

And thus it is with us today. Pioneering is not finished. There are great wildernesses of ignorance, injustice, untruth, apathy, poverty, hardship to be conquered. The untracked expanse lies all around us, waiting for strong arms, willing hands, understanding hearts, and iron wills to take up the burden where those earlier pioneers put it down. We must make for future generations a better world, as those who went before did for us.

Pioneering promises no life of ease, only satisfaction. We may wear ourselves out like the old man at the campfire; but we, like him, will rest with no regrets. The finest use of our lives is to spend them on something greater than ourselves.

The apostle Paul lived such a life. As he saw it drawing to a close, he left us these immortal words, "O death, where is thy sting? O grave, where is thy victory." (1 Corinthians 15:55.)

May we each go forth with an individual commitment to blaze noble trails that others may follow, and to improve the world wherever we go. May we work together in love and brotherhood; that we may sing as they sang a century and a quarter ago, "All is well! all is well!"

What Makes a
Good Leader

Dwight D. Eisenhower, who had opportunities to meet some of modern history's most eminent leaders, once catalogued the traits that to him made these men and women great. (See "What Is Leadership?" *Reader's Digest*, June 1965, pp. 51-53.) While outward personality styles may have been different, what was it, he asked, that stamped the minds and hearts of those souls destined to stand out and lead others? While most of us are merely marked by the world in which we live, sluggishly bending to every pressure, what was so special about those who came and instead left *their* marks?

What about Benjamin Franklin, the calm sage of the Continental Congress, who once sent 116 books to a small community to start a library? Horace Mann, who lived in that small community, became literate by reading those books, and in turn he stumped the country promoting free public education. It was largely his efforts that jolted the nation into opening school doors for even its poorest citizens. What about Louis Pasteur, Samuel F. B. Morse, Thomas A. Edison, Henry Ford? And just as important as these national figures, what about the nameless leaders who forged cities out of wildernesses, injected morale into tired communities, fought for causes that may not have always been popular?

We are blessed because of such leaders, and President Eisenhower tried to identify some of the qualities that infuse their shining hearts, qualities we ought to try to develop if we hope to have any personal effect on making our world a better place.

First, said Eisenhower, the leaders he observed possessed a single-minded and selfless dedication to the task at hand. They did not follow causes in order to puff up their personal standing. They were not endlessly asking what was in it for them. They saw their task as bigger than personal interests or discomforts. They took their job more seriously than they did themselves.

Too many would-be leaders undertake a mighty calling just to feed the needs of a hungry ego. Too many join organizations or committees merely to add a line to their resumeś. Some watch the clock and will not give the extra hours. Others weigh every move according to their own self-aggrandizement. Real leaders, said Eisenhower, let their cause predominate over themselves.

Second, leaders possess conviction and the courage to follow their ideals. Many people in the world merely imitate others and are frightened to walk an untried path, but leaders have such conviction in the justness and necessity of their cause that fear is dwarfed by higher motivations.

Leaders are not lukewarm about what they do. They do not study each task with a casual eye or form superficial opinions. Their task and their belief in their cause is as much a part of them as a beating heart. Christopher Columbus was bound to sail to America no matter how many royal rejections he received while wandering the European continent. Thomas A. Edison started to rebuild the morning after his laboratory burned down. Real leaders have conviction born of real study and emotion. They aren't just looking for something to do.

Third, real leaders have fortitude. Eisenhower described this as "the capacity to stand strong under reverses, to rise from defeat and do battle again, to learn from one's mistakes and push on to the ultimate goal." He wrote: "George Washington . . . is the classic American example of this quality. Except for one or two small triumphs, Washington was denied any important military victory until the final surrender of Cornwallis at Yorktown. However, the heartbreak of his 1776 battles around New York, the disappointments of Brandywine and Germantown, the bitter ordeal at Valley Forge, the neglect of his men by Congress and the States, the starvation, freezing and fighting, often with almost no weapons—all these he endured throughout the long years of the Revolution.

"Washington never even considered final defeat, and his conviction and devotion were so great that he pledged his entire private fortune to the cause of independence." (Ibid., pp. 51-52.)

Real leaders, then, do not let their fires be doused by the rain that falls into every life and on every cause.

Fourth, said Eisenhower, real leaders have the power of persuasion born of humility. They elicit the help and advice of their associates and subordinates. They recognize that coworkers need to feel a sense of creative achievement by helping the leader develop the program. They give credit where credit is due, allowing others the ultimate compliment of defined responsibilities and the reasonable freedom to execute them. And because others feel a sense of their own involvement in the program, the leader does not have to coerce them to accept his decisions. Those decisions are theirs too.

Fifth, said Eisenhower, leaders always do their homework. They do not hope to get by on a sleek image of a charismatic personality. Those are simply never enough.

Said he, "I never knew President Roosevelt as well as I did some of the other world leaders, but in the few conferences I had with him I was impressed, not only by his inspirational qualities, but by his amazing grasp of the whole complex war effort. He could discuss strategy on equal terms with his generals and admirals. His knowledge of the geography of the war theaters was so encyclopedic that the most obscure places in faraway countries were always accurately sited on his mental map. President Roosevelt possessed personality, surely, but as the nation's leader in a global conflict, he also did his homework—thoroughly." (Ibid., p. 53.)

So there they are, five qualities of leadership described by a man who ought to know: selfless dedication, conviction, fortitude, humility, and thorough homework. These are the leadership traits that not only get the job done, but also inspire others to want to get the job done. And these are the characteristics that can be employed in whatever level of leadership you find yourself, whether it be in upgrading the quality of education in your local school or upgrading the level of relationship around your own dinner table. Ask yourself: Do I care enough about this to forget myself and become absorbed in the task? Does successful completion of this goal fire me beyond casual purpose and gnawing fears? Can I get up every time I stumble while pursuing this job? Will I let others help, and am I willing to do my homework to accomplish this goal? When you can answer yes to these questions about the great cause or small job you hope to pursue, you are on your way to becoming an inspiring leader destined to make your corner of the world a better place.

You Can
Be a Champion

Let me introduce you to three champions. Every time Carl Joseph walks onto the football field, every time Pat Browne, Jr., splits the center of the fairway with a drive, and every time George Murray runs a race, be it a mile or a marathon, each is showing the kind of grit that the true champion is made of.

Carl Joseph won thirteen athletic letters in high school and now goes to college on a football scholarship. And he was born with only one leg.

Pat Browne, Jr., is an attorney and the president of a savings and loan company when he isn't playing championship golf and amazing the onlookers with trick golf shots. And Pat was blinded in an automobile accident six years ago.

George Murray not only competed in marathon races last year, but he also pushed himself all the way across America—in his wheelchair. (Dan Cody, "Neither Down nor Out," *Sky*, May 1982, p. 29.)

These three sports enthusiasts have something in common. It is not their so-called handicaps; rather it is their indomitable will, their refusal to let any obstacle take the fire out of their fighting spirits.

This kind of championship courage is not limited to the

athletic field, of course. We can find champions of this caliber everywhere if we look for them.

A friend of mine had been through the fighting in both Korea and Viet Nam. He had escaped bullets fired in anger, honorably served his career in the U.S. Air Force, and retired. Now he could finally be with his family and pursue the studies he loved. He went back to college, got his doctorate, and was beginning to enjoy the good things of life he had struggled so long to achieve and fought so hard to protect. Short months later, he was hit with an incurable paralysis that has left him completely helpless. He lies strapped to a breathing machine, fed through tubes and apparently imprisoned in his own body. He can hear, think, and move his eyes. That is all. What great cause he has to be bitter and resentful at the injustice life has handed him.

I went to see him again recently to cheer him up. As I looked into his eyes, do you know what I saw? An unmistakable twinkle. I saw a spirit inside that wasted body that would not be conquered. I went there to cheer him, but you know who got the biggest boost of our visit.

How do these people do it? How do they carry their burdens like cheerful champions when I can sometimes get thrown off balance by a broken shoelace? A big part of the secret, I am convinced, is in their attitude.

Kenneth Jernigan, president of the National Federation of the Blind, who is himself blind, said that blindness is not a handicap. It is only a characteristic, just as being tall, red-haired, or age twenty-five is a characteristic. Others disagree and say that blindness is not like other characteristics, because it brings with it great limitations. But Kenneth Jernigan counters by pointing out that every characteristic carries both opportunities and limitations.

He has a point. A tall person might be a good basketball player but a poor gymnast, where a compact muscular body is an advantage. A highly intelligent person might have an advantage in a classroom but a disadvantage in the job market, where employers might be afraid he would quickly grow bored and dissatisfied with the average job. The twenty-year-old might have more physical energy to get a job done, but the fifty-year-old might carry an air of authority that would be better to direct others in doing the work. In short, every aspect of life brings advantages and disadvantages.

This is not to belittle in any way those who have overcome physical, mental, economic, social, and other obstacles to accomplish their goals. Quite the contrary. It is to help us better understand what they know, take inspiration from what they have done, and go and do likewise.

This outlook is good for us in an additional way. It prevents us from looking at our own shortcomings and using them to justify our failings. It is so easy to say, "Oh, that's just the way I am. I'll never be able to improve." Or, "I have no talent in that area." Or worst of all, "The sin that I am committing is just a weakness I can't control." The message of these champions is that we are in control no matter what our outward circumstances may be.

I believe that is also the message of Jesus Christ in the parable of the talents. In the story, a lord went on a journey to a far country. He entrusted each of his three servants with varying amounts of money, called talents in those days. One had five talents, another two, and another one. Upon his return, the lord asked for an accounting of the talents. The servant with five talents had invested his and returned five more. The servant with two had done likewise and returned two more. Even though the second servant returned only half as much increase as the first, they both received the same commendation from their lord: "Well done, thou good and faithful servant."

It was the third servant who reaped his lord's condemnation. He had buried his talent and made no use of it. He had some fine rationalizations and reasons to explain his failure. He was afraid he might lose the talent. He was afraid of his lord. In the context of our discussion here, he might have added, "I was too small to make the team," or "I was too dumb to get good grades," or "I was psychologically unfit to face the world, so I had to rely on drink or drugs to get through the night," or "I have a weakness for women, so I am immoral," or "I never had a fair chance in life, and so I failed." The longest list in the history of the world could be compiled out of the excuses mankind has concocted to explain away the things that might have been but were not.

But all of the lazy servant's well-rehearsed rationalizations were swept away by his lord's stern rebuke: "Thou wicked and slothful servant." He then instructed his servants to take away the single talent from that servant and give it to another who could make better use of it. (Matthew 25: 14-30.)

The number of talents or the heavy burden of handicaps is not the deciding factor in success. Indeed, these may be a spur to those who refuse to give up. Would John Milton have developed his deep poetic insight if he had not been blind? Would Beethoven have heard celestial symphonies in his head if he had not been deaf? Would Franklin D. Roosevelt have developed his powerful, persuasive skills had he not been confined to a wheelchair? We cannot know, but this much we do know: each of these people and thousands more throughout history have used their so-called handicaps as springboards to achieve far beyond what was accomplished by the so-called normal people around them.

So follow these indomitable examples, search out the character weaknesses that might be holding you back, and go to work not only to overcome them, but to use them as your launching pad toward improvement and eventual perfection. In Paul's words: "Fight the good fight . . . lay hold on eternal life." (1 Timothy 6:12.)

The Example of Jesus the Man

Much has been written about Jesus Christ. Entire volumes have been devoted to specific aspects of His life, from the meaning of various statements to the mystical significance of His miracles. In fact, so much research and speculation concerning Him has been compiled that we may lose sight of Jesus as a person. Rather than seeing Him as a man, a friend or neighbor, an individual with the same feelings, needs, and aspirations as we have, we sometimes perceive Him as a historical figure, a lifeless subject for research or adoration.

The simple accounts of Jesus' life as presented in the New Testament, however, portray Jesus as a warm and uncomplicated person who lived an unpretentious and honest life.

In fact, if Jesus were alive today, He would be the type of person most of us would want to have as a close friend. With Him, we would be safe. There would be no conditions to the friendship. We would not have to be rich or learned; we would not have to live in a specific part of town or be of a particular race or creed. The sinners and publicans as well as the rich and famous were all candidates for His friendship.

And if you had a problem or misfortune, Jesus would be

the first to be concerned. When His friend and cousin John the Baptist was put in jail, Jesus inquired again and again about his welfare. And when His friend Lazarus died, Jesus wept.

Jesus was the type of person you'd choose as an employee or even as your own supervisor. He understood that people are more important than profit margins and company policies. When challenged by the Pharisees concerning the alleged breaking of one of the many policies instituted for Sabbath conduct, He responded: "The sabbath was made for man, and not man for the sabbath." (Mark 2:27.) Nor would you have to audit the books with Jesus in your employ. He would have no reason to steal, because during his mortal life he neither wanted nor needed anything beyond the basic necessities of life. "The labourer is worthy of his hire," He said. (Luke 10:7.) You could expect an honest day's work for an honest day's pay from this employee.

There would be no need for high fences if Jesus were your next-door neighbor. "Love thy neighbor" was His motto, and He lived by it. With Him, *love* was a verb, a word of action. To love our neighbor as He described it was to feed the hungry, to clothe the naked, to visit the sick. Being a neighbor to this man meant more than living close to someone; it meant treating others as you yourself would want to be treated.

If you knew Jesus today, you'd probably want Him to be your instructor in the adult-education program or teach your children in the public-school classroom. He taught using words and examples everyone could understand. He used illustrations from everyday life, from peoples' work and environment. When He taught individuals who had an agricultural background, for instance, He used examples they would understand. He talked about sheep and cattle, seeds and wheat. Best of all, He told lots of stories when He taught—simple stories, uplifting stories, stories with a purpose. And He loved children. Once when He was giving a talk and some youngsters were making noise, as all children do, He brought them to the front so they could hear better. He even said that the kingdom of heaven would be filled with childlike people.

Another quality Jesus had was sensitivity to or fondness for living things, a reverence for life and for all creatures. He talked about freeing a cow that was stuck in the mud, even if you were wearing your good clothes and were on the way to church. When He drove the money changers out of the temple, He first freed the doves, so they wouldn't get hurt in the ensuing commotion.

Jesus was a simple man. He never wore fancy clothes; He didn't live in an extravagant house or eat gourmet food. He never belonged to any national organizations or clubs. His dress was simple; His manners were simple; His entire life was simple.

Like His life, the teachings of Jesus were simple and unfettered by complicated dogma or mysticism. To do good was his religion—to do good in all the places that He could, whenever He could, to whomever He could. But the simplicity of Jesus was not just the plainness of nonextravagance. That grand simplicity which results in singleness of purpose directed Him through His ministry and along the long road to Calvary.

Yes, His miracles and His claim to divine parenthood were authentic. He was what He claimed to be: the Son of God. And it is this very fact that makes His life of love and charity so important to all who call themselves after His name.

To be a good neighbor, a sincere friend, a sensitive human being; to live simply and honestly—these are the distinctions of a true child of God.

Let No Man Despise Thy Youth

"Youth is so wonderful, it is a shame to waste it on the young." So said George Bernard Shaw, the famous playwright and wit. Whether or not youth is wasted on the young is one man's opinion, but there is no question that it is a marvelous time.

Our culture has been so smitten by the glories of youth that we seem bent on turning every age into another trip through the teens. One rather mature gentleman had a face lift, hair transplant, and tummy tuck, and was pouring another bottle of tint into his gray locks when one of his friends said, "You know what, you're not going to be satisfied until you break out in acne."

Sports and entertainment stars are often heroes and has-beens before they're hardly out of high school. We are constantly cajoled to look and behave young as though there were something vaguely obscene about a gray hair or a wrinkle. But this imagined imitation of youth is not quite the same thing as respect, and that is the subject of this discussion.

Youth does, of course, have its pitfalls, as does any phase of life, and those of more mature years feel fully qualified to enumerate those foibles. Youth can be impetuous, inconsiderate, long on action and short on judgment, unappreciative, easily misled, wayward, and a long list of other real and imagined shortcomings.

But maturity has its problems as well, and one of these is wringing its hands and claiming the kids are going to the canines. This tendency to tick off lists of the foibles of youth and write off the perpetrators thereof is not a new phenomenon. Almost two thousand years ago Paul wrote to his young friend Timothy, "Let no man despise thy youth; but be thou an example of the believers." (1 Timothy 4:12.)

We may sometimes despise or discount the youth among us, but the Lord surely does not. The prophet Samuel in the Old Testament found this out when he went on his assignment from the Lord to find a new king for Israel. Samuel apparently had fixed in his mind the image of a proper king as he approached the house of Jesse, to whom he had been sent. Israel's new king would be wise of stature with a noble brow, a wise face etched with a respectable number of wrinkles from solving profound problems, and a mature mind with which to lead the armies and guide the government of the Lord's people.

And so Samuel tried to match the image in his mind with the sons of Jesse as they passed by him one by one, from the oldest down to the youngest. But the voice of the Lord whispered to Samuel that the king was not among them. Samuel, somewhat confused, asked Jesse if these were all the sons he had. Jesse replied, almost as an afterthought, "There remaineth yet the youngest, and, behold, he keepeth the sheep." The prospect of a shepherd boy presiding over the kingdom was farfetched, but Samuel had few other options at this point. And so the youngest son was brought in. The fair-haired boy with the beautiful voice and the beardless, unwrinkled face was far from what Samuel had in mind, but the heavenly whisper confirmed that this was indeed the man.

It was not long until that choice was vindicated in the valley of Elah. This stripling stood up when the bravest of Israel's warriors would not. He slew the giant Goliath and later became Israel's most renowned king, David. (1 Samuel 16–17.)

No, we cannot despise, discredit, or discount a man or woman because of a lack of years. Some of the most famous persons in scripture and history were hardly more than children when they began their work. Samuel was just a boy when a heavenly voice called to him in the temple. Joseph was sold into Egypt at the age of seventeen; Jeremiah was called near the age of thirteen; and, of course, the Lord Jesus Christ, as a boy of twelve, was found by His parents in the temple amazing the learned doctors and scribes with His intelligence and knowledge.

Joseph Smith was a lad of fourteen when he began his work. He was ridiculed by those who could not believe a boy could be called to such a responsibility. Yet today, more than a century and a half later, long after the names of his detractors are lost to history, Joseph Smith is revered as a prophet by more than five million Mormons throughout the world.

Youth with its boundless energy and propensity for passionate involvement can do marvelous works in the world. But that power is a two-edged sword. Youth can also be led or misled. More than one demagogue and tyrant has tapped the power of youth to further his evil designs. Hitler's brownshirted youth groups, Mussolini's Black Shirts, and the Young Communist League in Russia are sad examples.

But lack of leadership can be equally detrimental to young people. Left alone without direction and example, they can stumble and do themselves and society great harm. The burning, looting, and rioting of the 1960s were committed largely by youths who marched under the slogan that they were a generation apart and would have no truck with adults over thirty. What they were really saying was that they had been abandoned by those who should have guided, counseled, and loved them.

When we separate the energy of youth from the wisdom of maturity, both generations suffer. The best compliment we can pay to youth is to join them in their quest for knowledge, wisdom, and a better world. This doesn't mean trying to turn back the clock, but it does mean keeping our enthusiasm high and nourishing a willingness to learn and grow just as we expect them to.

We would do well to follow these observations of Samuel Johnson. He said, "I love the acquaintance of young people; because . . . I don't like to think of myself growing old." George Santayana put it this way, "Never have I enjoyed youth so thoroughly as I have in my old age. . . . Nothing is inherently and invincibly young except spirit. And spirit can enter a human being perhaps better in the quiet of old age and dwell there more undisturbed than in the turmoil of adventure."

So let us bridge whatever gaps may separate us and use the best that each of us has to make this a better world for the aged, the mature, the youth, and the child, as well as for the generations yet unborn that will follow us.

A Modest Cheer for
the Later Years

I looked out the window this morning and was mildly surprised to see that this year was maturing and shortly would be drawing to a close. Such things do creep up on us. But the harvest of this year, literally and figuratively, has been good. The experiences, the work, the joys, and even the sorrows have made it a good year. I do not mourn its passing. I have enjoyed it. And I hope I will continue to say that as the years progress. I like Bernard Baruch's observation. He said, "Old age is always fifteen years older than I am." We seem to shun the idea of age in our society, but other cultures don't feel that way.

In Korea old men dress neatly in white clothes with black hats and gather on street corners in the cities. There they talk among themselves, but their most important function is to be available if younger people come for information and advice. What a splendid idea, I thought when I heard that. No big deal, no formal meetings of elaborate preparations, just the generations meeting on a street corner. In Korea, a country that has long venerated its older people, it is assumed that the experience of the elders will be of value to younger generations.

This is perhaps a hard concept to grasp in this dynamic,

dashing, up-to-date world in which we live. We are admonished to think young, act young, behave young, and be young. I sometimes wonder if this perennial pursuit is a heritage left over from the first explorers who came to America looking for the fountain of youth. We have never really given up the search.

Youth is a marvelous time. None of us would quarrel with that statement. In youth, body and mind are vigorous, growing, and developing. New ideas and experiences pop up every day. It is a glorious time.

But youth is not the only glorious time of life. Maturity and the later years have their joys and satisfactions as well. Returning to the Orient for a bit of wisdom, it is said that if a person in China asks your age and you give him a figure less than fifty, he will shake his head consolingly and say, "Don't feel bad, you'll get there one of these years," or similar words of condolence. The idea of surviving half a century is a noble aspiration to the Chinese, a proud thing to achieve.

In America we seem to be more intrigued and entertained by the accomplishments of youth. There is no doubt that today's youth are an impressive generation. Olympic athletes are doing in their early teens what we used to think only a mature man or woman could accomplish. Brilliant scholars are whipping through college and launching their careers by the time many are just getting the hang of how to register for high school. These are exciting lives to observe.

But for every child prodigy we see, we can point to an inspirational story of an older person who helped shape the world.

Alexander the Great conquered the world before he was twenty-five, but his teacher, a much older man, has affected world history more profoundly. That teacher was half a century old before anyone ever heard of him, yet today, after two and a half millennia, the western world still looks back to take its bearings from the wisdom of the learned Aristotle.

Then there was the politician who was virtually un-known until past his fiftieth birthday, but who, in his final five years, held together the crumbling foundation of the na-tion—the immortal Abraham Lincoln.

Remember the man who was into his eighth decade when he helped steer the minds of those young men who hammered out the United States Constitution? What form of government would we have had without the wisdom of the venerable Benjamin Franklin?

Yes, the history books are full of people who refused to accept their mature or even declining years as a wasted, burned-out derelict time of life.

Perhaps more significant than the famous figures are the millions of men and women who will never be known ex-cept to their families and friends. But those who love them will rise up to call their names blessed because they guided, led, helped, counseled, and advised from the benefit of their experience.

Sometimes we are misled by outward appearances. We see the lines that age puts on our faces, and we dread the coming of the years. But while youthful beauty can be breathtaking, the serene beauty of a life well lived can move the soul more deeply. I am reminded of the words of John Donne: "No spring, nor summer beauty hath such grace, /As I have seen in one autumnal face." (*Elegy* ix, "The Au-tumnal," l.i.)

But aren't older people limited physically? Well, yes, I suppose so, but that doesn't mean they have died inside. They may be quietly savoring those deeper joys that can come only with the enriching of the years. They may not need much diversion and personal gratification. Rather they are finding joy in helping others. I talked with a man a while ago who had had a brilliant career in sports. He had been an all-around high school athlete, then had played professional baseball. He had heard that satisfying crack of his bat as he belted one over the fence; had executed that brilliant bit of fielding that brings fans to their feet; had heard the roar of the crowd on his behalf; had felt the flush of victory many times. Now he was coaching a youth team. He told me, "I never thought I would get a greater thrill out of seeing kids I coached excel than I did out of playing myself, but that's how I feel now."

That, I believe, is the payment for learning the lessons that only age and experience can bring us. Maturity can bring a warm glow and sense of satisfaction that youth can only savor momentarily as it hurries to accomplish all the personal victories that seem so important at that age.

So let us not be afraid of the advancing years. Let us accept the wrinkles and bless the twinkles that age brings. In the life well lived, every scene of the unfolding drama should be savored; as in a well-crafted play, the final acts should be the culmination of the prologues that have gone before. As Job said many years ago, "With the ancient is wisdom; and in length of days understanding." (Job 12:12.)

The Lord Is on Our Side

In a time of war you would think it extremely strange if the general in charge of the army deliberately reduced his forces and sent men home before the battle. And you would think the reduction even stranger if the opposing army were massive and ready to attack. But surprisingly, that is just what the Lord told Gideon to do in one of the most remarkable stories in all of scripture.

When the Children of Israel entered the promised land after years of wandering in the desert, they had many battles to fight to claim the land as their own. In one such battle, the Israelite army led by Gideon was opposing the Midianites, an army so large they looked like grasshoppers standing along the edge of the valley. Even their camels, say the scriptures, were without number. The Israelites, for their part, had thirty-two thousand men, another great host.

Just before the swords were about to clash, the Lord did an interesting thing. He said to Gideon, "The people that are with thee are too many for me." What? Gideon must have wondered if he'd heard right. But the Lord told him He wanted a smaller army and to send home anyone who was afraid. Twenty-two thousand men gladly left, leaving ten thousand to fight the war.

Again the Lord said to Gideon, "The people are yet too many," and he asked Gideon to winnow them further. When the process was completed, only a trembling three hundred men were left to go against the Midianite army that stood like insects across from them. (Judges 7:1-8.)

Had the Lord diminished the army to reduce Israel's chances of winning? No. The issue was not really *if* Israel won; rather it was *why* they won. He told Gideon that only with a pitifully small army would Israel remember that the Lord had won the battle that day for them; they had not won it for themselves. They needed a graphic demonstration of their dependence on Him. After all, it was their own parents who had earlier told Moses, "My power and the might of mine hand hath gotten me this wealth." (Deuteronomy 8:17.)

Centuries have passed since that battle. Cultures and governments have come and gone, but human nature remains surprisingly the same. Most of us believe that life is a do-it-yourself experience, and we are insulted to ask anyone, even the Lord, for help. To admit need is to admit weakness, so we say to ourselves, "My brilliance is responsible for this idea," or "My own hands pulled me through this time," or "My eyes see all that is important in the world," or "My brain comprehends all necessary things."

We retain that stubborn immaturity we sometimes see in children, who will refuse help when they desperately need it, saying, "I'll do it myself."

But as one writer said, "Your ultimate achievements in this life will be determined more by your ability to pull down the powers of heaven upon yourself than reliance on your natural abilities." (Grant Von Harrison, *Drawing on the Powers of Heaven*, Accord Publishing Co., 1982, p. viii.) It is impossible to realize our ultimate potential in this world without the Lord's help.

President Ezra Taft Benson said, "Men and women who turn their lives over to God will find out that he can make a lot more out of their lives than they can. He will deepen their joys, expand their vision, quicken their minds, strengthen their muscles, lift their spirits, multiply their blessings, increase their opportunities, comfort their souls, raise up friends, and pour out peace." (Ibid.) That's quite a promise; yet many of us grovel in the dust because we refuse to recognize what the Lord can do for us.

Those who are great among us are often great because they have learned to call upon the Lord and make his help effective in their lives. They have pulled down the powers of heaven to enhance their own faltering abilities. President J. Reuben Clark, Jr., one of the top leaders in the Church and an eminent legal mind, was asked at one time to teach a Sunday School class in his ward. Knowing that he was tremendously busy, the Sunday School officers told him, "You don't need to attend prayer meeting if you will just be there to teach the class." President Clark told them he would be glad to take the class, but only if he could attend the prayer meeting. He knew he could not teach unless he participated in the prayer and gained the spirit, strength, and support of the Lord.

We all need that support. The world is full of do-gooders who do little good because they don't penetrate to the secret of the individual human heart. The Lord could reveal to them the unspoken need of another and the principles of happiness, but they just assume they know, and they plough ahead without help. The world is full of parents who search the books of experts for help in rearing their children, and don't consult the expert who's been a Father for eternities. The world is full of dreamers whose visions are shattered when they strain against the limits of their own talents.

We are all like the Israelite army, for we constantly need to be reminded who wins our battles for us. Unfortunately, however, most of us wait until life has driven us to our knees before we kneel there of our own accord. We wait until life seems to have ganged up upon us before we cry for help. When someone we love is desperately ill, or we are in the trenches of reality and bombs are exploding overhead, or life seems so immense and depressing that we don't want to get out of bed in the morning, we finally say, "Where are you?" Perhaps the Lord even lets us get into that position so we can at last hear him say, "Come unto me."

No matter who we are or how heavily the balance seems weighed against us, we can overcome. No matter how powerful our enemies or how desperate our plight, we do not need to fight alone. One soul and the Lord are always a majority.

If to our view the world seems pitted in a conspiracy to make us fail, if our hearts are faint when they ought to be strong, if our vision fails us and our optimism wanes, we can be sure we have not learned to call effectively upon the Lord for help. We have not learned how to use him on our side.

How do we finally do that? It takes exertion. It takes humility. It takes remembering that we are all born naked and ignorant and are dependent on him for every good thing. Most of all, it takes leaning on him just as much when the harvest is in and the bins are full as when the bin is empty and the world is a place without warmth or security.

The Lord is on our side as he was with the straggly Israelite army. The only thing that will circumscribe his acting in our behalf are the barriers we ourselves raise when we say, "I have no need of thee. I can do it myself."

May we be great enough to learn that we cannot be truly great without the Lord.

They That Be with Us

You know the feeling (I guess we all do)—that groggy moment just when you are coming out of a sound sleep. Your eyelids weigh about sixty pounds apiece, the covers are cosy, and the mattress has a firm grip on your back. For a couple of minutes you couldn't lick your weight in pillow feathers. It's not the moment to take on big new projects—like facing a ferocious army, for example.

So picture yourself in the place of Elisha in the Old Testament as his servant burst through the door to tell him that they were surrounded by the armed hosts of the Syrians.

Elisha got up and took a look around. There stood the soldiers just as his servant had said, armed to the teeth and ready to chew up anything in their path. That sort of greeting first thing in the morning can really ruin your day. But Elisha looked out on the scene with an eye of faith, and he saw something that had escaped the panicky glance of his fearful servant. Surrounding the army was another and even more numerous army of heavenly protectors, whom Elisha described as "an host . . . with horses and chariots." He turned to his trembling servant and said, "Fear not: for they that be with us are more than they that be with them." (2 Kings 6:15-16.)

As a testimony of this truth, the attacking army was

struck blind and retreated in disarray. And Elisha went back to the work that he had been called to as a prophet.

Most of us won't face anything as fearsome as an invading army the first thing in the morning, but sometimes it can seem that way. And not just in the morning, of course, but off and on throughout the day, the week, and the year, we are hit with challenges and problems that can overwhelm us. We are surrounded and beset upon, hampered, hindered, and threatened by the forces of opposition. And like Elisha's servant, there may be times when all we can see is the enemy.

At such times we would be well advised to follow Elisha's lead: to look closer and see if there are not also friendly allies surrounding and waiting to help us. They may or may not be the armed angels of Elisha, but they will surely be there.

Where will they come from, these allies who will assist us? Some of them will come from those who care about us, neighbors, friends, and members of our family who, seeing our need, will respond in surprising ways. Sometimes it may only be a word of encouragement, but that may be enough. The Greek philosopher Epicurus made that point when he wrote, "We do not so much need the help of our friends as the confidence of their help in need." Sometimes just the assurance that our friends are there is enough to get us over a rough spot.

Another source of strength we need to make the best use of is the kind of which Sidney J. Phillips spoke: "Men are made stronger on realization that the helping hand they need is at the end of their own right arm."

Great power is found in each of us. We certainly have not yet fathomed the potential of the human mind or even the human body. What strong men once did, little girls apparently can do today. Recently a 46-pound girl who was in the fourth grade lifted 450 pounds. Achievements that thirty years ago won Olympic gold medals now would not even qualify one for a place on the team. No, we do not know what the human body can do.

And what is said of the body goes tenfold for the human mind and spirit. It is said, and truly so, that anything the mind can conceive and believe, it can achieve.

Believing in this case does not mean just paying lip service to a fantasy. It means believing until it becomes an integral part of our subconscious, the wellsprings of our actions, so that our goals guide, direct, and motivate everything we do. With this kind of belief and faith, virtually anything is possible.

People once believed that man would never fly, certainly that he would never break the bands of his earthly habitation and soar beyond the force of gravity into the stars. Yet we're all acquainted with the success of the space programs.

Closer to earth, there are those who scoff and say, "Yes, with incredible power packed into a rocket, a man might ride along as a passenger, but he would never fly under his own power." But recently a man flew across the English Channel in a pedal-powered plane with nothing but his legs to make it go. A humble effort, of course, in comparison with moon flight, but then so was Kitty Hawk.

Yes, there is great power within our minds and bodies, and it is multiplied when others come to our aid. But even so, we will find times when our combined strength is not equal to the task.

If we are trying to do good, we may rest assured that opposition will rise up to meet us, and sometimes it may almost overwhelm us. At such times, let us not forget the greatest power of all that we can call on—help from heaven. It may not appear in the form of Elisha's armed angels, but it will be there, and it will be sufficient to our needs. We will know of a surety within our hearts that "they that be with us are more than they that be with them."

The Power of
Imagination

Mary Chase wrote a Broadway play a few years ago that has become a classic. The title character is one of the most famous personages ever to appear on the Broadway stage. He was a delightful, witty, insightful, ofttimes profound protagonist who stood a full six feet tall in his furry feet. He also had two unusual qualities that set him apart from other Broadway stars: he was a rabbit, and he was invisible. But these two eccentricities have not kept him from being a vivid and vibrant memory in the lives of everyone who has ever seen the play.

The memorable character's name was Harvey. Originally Harvey was to have been a real, live actor dressed in a bunny suit. But the producer had a stroke of inspiration during the last rehearsals of the play. He decided that rather than limit us to his conception of what a six-foot wizened rabbit would look like, he would let us use the power of our own imaginations to create our own Harvey. This inspiration, in the words of columnist Sidney Harris, "turned a mildly amusing play into a masterpeice of whimsey." (*Deseret News*, February 5, 1982.) Harvey the rabbit is only another in a long list of well-known people and places that you and I have known and visited on the magic ticket of our imaginations. Those who go back to the golden age of radio drama will remember Amos and Andy, Fibber McGee's closet, and the spine-chilling sounds from the *Inner Sanctum* mystery series. The characters and scenes were as real to us as the rooms in which we sat and laughed or shivered in fright.

Radio developed a far more faithful following than has television. One reason for that is what Stan Freberg once said when commenting on the difference between the two media: "Radio expands the mind." A straight man to this famous humorist said, "But doesn't television expand the mind?" Freberg replied, "Up to twenty-one inches, yes." (Radio commerical produced by Radio Advertising Bureau.) This is not an advertisement for radio over television, but it is a hearty endorsement for the powers of your marvelous imagination. Through the power of your imagination, you can create not only the make-believe world of theater and drama, but in a large measure the real world in which you live. In fact, there has been some spirited debate about the differences between the so-called real world and the interpretations of the world we create in our minds.

No less an insightful observer than Shakespeare declared, "All the world's a stage, /And all the men and women merely players." (*As You Like It*, II, vii, 139.) There is much truth in that. Maxwell Maltz, a noted plastic surgeon, found that he could change the appearances of people: take away their warts and blemishes, rearrange their odd-shaped features, and give them handsome, beautiful faces. Yet he found that changing the outward appearance had virtually no effect on the success and the happiness of his patients. It was not until he got involved with their inner selves and helped them change their self-perceptions, their view of themselves and their world—their imagination, if you will—that his outward beautification began to have any effect on them. Such is the power of our inner mind.

What many people don't seem to realize is that the marvelous blessing of imagination is a gift to each of us from our Creator. Our imagination belongs to us. We can create all the heroic scenes and happy endings we could ever wish for right inside the theater of our minds. But far too often, we prefer stage tragedies, with ourselves in the title role. And then we call this the "real" world.

The truth is that body and mind rarely, if ever, react to the so-called real world, but rather to interpretations of information from environment that the senses send to the brain.

In a large city late one night, I had to make a phone call. I found a telephone booth, but I wished the street were better lighted, having heard many stories about attacks and muggings in our cities. But I took a chance anyway. As I finished my call and turned to leave the phone booth, standing just outside was a rather shadowy, ominous-looking figure. I pushed open the folding doors of the phone booth and hoped I could brush right by him and be on my way. But suddenly I saw his arm raised toward me. Instantly my body stiffened, the adrenalin poured into my bloodstream, my muscles tightened, and my heart began to palpitate. This was real danger, and my body was getting ready for it.

In the next instant my shadowy attacker reached out not for me, but for the telephone-booth door, which he wanted to open. Then I saw under the brim of his hat the kindly and surprised face of an elderly gentleman who probably wondered what kind of nervous rabbit had jumped out of the "bushes" of the telephone booth.

Later, I was finally able to chuckle to myself. I remembered Shakespeare's line, ". . . in the night imagining some fear, how easy is a bush suppos'd a bear." (*A Midsummer's Night's Dream*, V, i, 18.) The point is, that confrontation was real to every system in my body, although it did not exist in the outside world.

How many other similar confrontations have I created? How many scenes of frustration or defeat have I generated in my mind that have caused my whole mind, heart, and body to respond, simply because I misinterpreted outside signals from that so-called real world?

The imagination and the mind have such power over the body that if we can interpret scenes of danger or anxiety or frustration or defeat, then we can also create scenes of success, satisfaction, happiness, pride—all the good things that the Lord has given us in this good life we live in.

An old truth that needs repeating every day of our lives was expressed well by John Milton more than three hundred years ago. He wrote, "The mind is its own place, and in itself can make a heav'n of hell, a hell of heav'n."

So go forth and tap the incredible energy, power, and ability of the mind that God has given you, and begin to create your own personal heaven right here on earth.

The Chance to Fail

We hear a lot in our world about successful people. Now for a minute, let's talk about failures. I have four specifically in mind: a businessman, a scientist, a politician, and a lawyer. Each of them failed as miserably as you and I could if we deliberately set out to do so.

The businessman had a thriving retail store that expanded into a chain, and soon he was a millionaire many times over. He was competent, worked hard, knew his business well, and had the extra sense of how to move ahead of the competition, all of which marked him for success from the very beginning. But he was not perfect, as none of us are; and in the midst of his great success, he made a costly miscalculation. As a result, he was soon bankrupt and out of business.

The second man aspired to the life of an intellectual. But he was slow, inattentive, nonconforming, an academic failure. His parents finally shuttled him off to Switzerland, where he would not be a disgrace to the family; and after his schooling, he got an obscure job among the gray ranks of the government bureaucracy. As a brilliant intellectual, he was a pretty good patent examiner.

The third man failed in the classic proportions that only

politicians have the resources to accomplish. In World War I
when the allied forces were very hard pressed, he came up
with what he thought would be a brilliant naval maneuver
that would hasten the war's end in one bold stroke. Instead
the whole affair was a fiasco, a crushing blow to his country
and to the allied cause.

The fourth man was a lawyer, and eventually a pretty
good one, though he started out in poor circumstances. Had
he been content to stay with his practice, he would have been
a recognized success in his community. His failure lay in aspiring to be a leader as well as a lawyer. He had aspirations
to be a statesman and thought he could make a contribution
to his country. But he was one of a small minority who felt
that way. He was defeated in election after election. He did
win a seat to Congress for one term, but then his electorate
was apparently unsatisfied with his performance. Again, as
a statesman, he was a pretty good lawyer.

Failures—the world is full of them. Every contest that
declares a winner declares in the same breath any number of
losers. There are not enough trophies to hand out to all who
try, and if we proliferate the prizes, we only make them
meaningless. Failure seems to be built into the system of our
world. We all fail. If we go through life without a failure, it
only means we have aspired too low.

But failure seems to go against the good old American
spirit of winning and "can do." Wouldn't it have been better
if the businessman could have avoided his fateful miscalculation that cost him a whole life's work? Wouldn't it have
been kinder of the fates to give our scientific intellectual a
few more obvious academic skills so he could have sat at the
front of the class where he aspired to be?

Wouldn't many lives have been spared had our statesman general had a better plan in World War I? And wouldn't
it have been better if our lawyer had spent a lifetime in gov-

ernment service rather than merely building up a reasonably successful private practice?

From our limited perspective, we might have set up the world in that way. But had we done so, the results would have been less beneficial for these four persons or for the world.

The business leader who went broke said that had he not, he would never have found the Lord, redirected his life, and rebuilt his retail chain on a commitment to serve his fellowmen. Millions of people have been better served because of the character thus built in the life of J. C. Penney.

Our aspiring scientist might have been catapulted to immediate intellectual stardom. He might have led his class and then gone on into a comfortable academic chair at some famous university. But without the intellectual exile he endured, would he have developed the independence of thought that later restructured our view of the entire universe? Would he have been the same Albert Einstein?

Our politician and would-be military genius cost himself and his British homeland dearly by his failure in the Dardanelle campaign in World War I. But without that failure and others, would he have been the pillar of unconquerable strength who defied the Nazi war machine and inspired his people to fight on? The maps of our present world might read much differently had he not been previously tried and tempered by fire, this British Prime Minister, Winston Churchill.

So also with our aspiring lawyer. By the time he was finally elected, he had honed his humanity on the whetstone of failure. Even in his success, his was a minority mandate made possible only by the splintering of the other parties. His administration was less than a dazzling success. His policies split the union. His cabinet carped and criticized him. He was pictured by the press as a public buffoon. His generals fumbled and stumbled, and with a vastly superior force he could not bring the war to a close for more than four long years. Yet out of this failure came one of the greatest humanitarians and inspiring leaders the world has ever seen. His great soul and sinewy frame held the nation together through its darkest hour. Without his early failures, would he have been the same Abraham Lincoln?

We are fond of saying that nothing succeeds like success, but often nothing succeeds like a setback if it is handled properly and viewed in the proper perspective. Thus we must each see our struggle in a longer view, and look toward the eternity that is our future. Only then can we estimate the results of our efforts.

One of the great failures in history from the view of his contemporaries would have been that man whose dreams were discredited, whose work was ridiculed, who was betrayed and abandoned by his closest supporters, and who was ignominiously executed as a criminal on the hill at Golgotha. But from the viewpoint of eternity, He is the hope for the success and salvation of us all.

Keep Love in Your Marriage

Not long ago Mike and Catherine Hauk of Terry, Montana, went dancing. Like Eliza Doolittle in *My Fair Lady*, they "could have danced all night." And they did dance more than five hours. He looked deep into her eyes and she into his as they swayed gently to the music. They were in love, and everybody knew it. But nobody but themselves knew how deeply in love they were.

Oh, the townfolk had some idea, and those who heard them repeat their marriage vows earlier in the evening were no doubt impressed with their sincerity to love and keep and care for one another in sickness and in health. But even they couldn't know how much Mike and Catherine meant what they said, for the sparkle-eyed couple in love were repeating promises they had made to each other back in 1912. Among those watching this seventieth wedding anniversary ceremony were seventy-one descendents—children, grandchildren, great-grandchildren, and great-great-grandchildren.

The family and friends dried their eyes, shook hands all around, and then Mike took his sweetheart dancing as he had most every Saturday night since this century was barely a decade old. (*Deseret News*, October 18, 1982, p. A-2.)

Mike and Catherine can give us all a lesson in love. In our fast-and-fancy, hurry-in-and-hurry-out, free-and-easy, do-your-own-thing society, many people have developed strange and sometimes selfish notions about what constitutes true love. They have the mistaken idea that there is really only one kind of romance: white-hot flame that streaks like an electric arc between two people who share some magical mix of conductive chromosomes. Fiery, uncontrollable, master of every other thought and feeling, wild and untamed—that is the love we sing and write about. And when it doesn't happen, or when the electric tingle settles down a bit, we grow disappointed and wonder where the romance went.

In reality, love is much more like a growing, living plant than an explosive, bursting fire. It needs gentle sowing to begin with, then fertile soil and a proper climate in which to grow. And, like any worthwhile and beautiful thing, it needs time to flower into its most nearly perfect form.

This is a lesson that needs repeating over and over again today.

In America, where almost half of the people who love each other enough to take the vows of matrimony later find themselves in the pain and misery of a divorce court, we apparently need lessons in love. These people did not set out to deliberately hurt themselves, their chosen mates, children, and others who got caught and ground up in the heart-rending and stomach-wrenching pain of divorce. They loved each other once; that's why they got married. But they let their love starve. They did not nourish it. A fire will grow cold without fuel; a plant will wither without nourishment; and love will die if it is ignored.

Dr. Paul E. Dahl, a marriage counselor, gave the following seven assignments to help us keep the love in marriage. I commend them to you.

Assignment number one: Strengthen your relationship with your Father in heaven. Richard Lovelace wrote a poem that ends with these famous lines, "I could not love thee, dear, so much, / Lov'd I not honor more." ("Wars," st. 3.) The same might be said of love for your Father in heaven. You can love each other more when you love Him. As you learn to love and serve Him and His children, your fellowmen, you will grow and mature into more unselfish and caring individuals. Then your love for one another in marriage will become a beautiful, mutually growing relationship and not the sad story of two selfish and sick souls clinging together for support against the world.

Assignment number two: Spend time together. Somebody commented on the old adage, "Absence makes the heart grow fonder," and added, "for somebody else." In this busy world of appointments, meetings, schedules, and assignments, don't forget to schedule some time for the most important person in your life. What is sadder than to see a husband and wife, when the dust has settled from the hectic pace of career and children, who then look at each other across the breakfast table and see almost a stranger sitting there?

Assignment number three: Listen to each other. Nowhere is listening more important than in marriage.

Assignment number four: Develop a friendship with your spouse. Does that sound strange? I wish it didn't. Unfortunately this is a step in love that is often overlooked. But a friend is one you like to be with, to share your inner thoughts and feelings with. You think of a friend's needs even before your own, and you value a friend's opinion. Friendship is a solid foundation upon which to build and maintain a beautiful edifice of love.

Assignment number five: Do something special for each other every day. This doesn't have to be a dozen long-stemmed roses or breakfast in bed. A phone call, a love note in his lunch box or on her pillow, a specially thought-out compliment can cover a multitude of mistakes and even an occasional forgotten anniversary.

Assignment number six: Share new and special insights and experiences. Here again, this doesn't have to be Paris in the springtime. It can be the sunset from your back porch or a book from the library. It's the sharing, not the size of the adventure, that counts.

Assignment number seven: Take a second or third or fourth honeymoon. Get away from the rest of the world for a little while and remind each other why you fell in love. You will probably find that true love, like great music and literature, grows deeper and more profound with time. Each time you return to it, it seems to have an added luster. The notes or the words have not changed, but you will bring deeper understanding and appreciation to what was always there. Let your love grow into this, and it will never turn old and stale. ("Keeping Your Marriage Alive," *Ensign*, July 1982, pp. 56-60.)

And when the going gets a little rough, take each other in your arms and remember Mike and Catherine Hauk dancing through three quarters of a century.

Keep God's Unchanging Laws

In the past twenty-five years our culture has changed radically in regard to sexual behavior. We have rushed head-long like a kamikaze pilot into the so-called new morality, a grim outlook that dishes us a daily diet of sexual innuendo wherever we turn. The idea is that physical intimacy is just an appetite like any other and is governed by no special moral law. Silly ads try to sell their products by reminding the user that this cologne or that toothpaste will increase sex appeal. Cheap magazines are commonly available. Television shows and movies are heavily loaded with sex-oriented material.

One young child asked her mother if movies now were like that when she was a little girl. When the mother said no, the child replied, "Oh, Mom, you were lucky."

Anyone who doubts that we're in the middle of an ethical earthquake that is toppling old standards need only see the statistics. From 1957 to 1977 the percentage of unwed mothers in this country tripled. Young people are facing many pressures and temptations that can demoralize them. Surprisingly, when a survey was done among teenagers about why they engaged in immoral behavior, the answers had little to do with passion. Instead they said such things as pressure from peers, everybody's doing it, fear of losing a boyfriend by refusal, loneliness, desperate need for company, and defiance of parents.

In other words, immoral sexual behavior seems to be the fad of our day, and many children submit themselves to it simply to belong. We can pick up a fashion magazine from forty years ago and laugh at the clothes then considered stylish. We wonder how anyone could have been persuaded to wear baggy pants or pompadours. We laugh that a few could say what color was in for the spring, what hairstyle. But if we analyze it, behavior is in that same realm. Lifestyles go in and out of popularity and acceptance; and while we may feel highly superior to some belief of another time, we are often caught by equally silly beliefs of our own day. Today our whole culture is being victimized by loose sexual ideas that have become widely accepted. And as has been the case with other cultures before us that have embraced false notions, our society will be led to folly and misery by sexual immorality.

The reason for this is simple. Moral behavior cannot be determined by whatever seems popular at any given time. It is based on eternal law. President Spencer W. Kimball has said, "God is the same yesterday, today, and forever. He has never intended that we should change or update with our vision the moral issues which he established long ago. Sin is still sin and always will be. We stand for a life of cleanliness. From childhood through youth and to the grave, we proclaim the wickedness of sexual life of any kind before marriage, and we proclaim that everyone in marriage should hold himself or herself to the covenants that we made. In other words, . . . there should be total chastity of men and women before marriage and total fidelity in marriage." (*Ensign*, November 1975, pp. 6-7.)

God is not whimsical, changing with the breeze of public opinion. He has given us unchanging laws because these are the principles that, if followed, will make us happy. He knows how easy it is for us to be victims of the latest opinions, and He gives us something steady to hold on so we are not duped and misled into anguish.

Human sexuality is a gift from God, created by Him to bind together two who are married. It is sacred when used within its proper context, but its abuse can cause no end of unhappiness. Participants in immoral behavior lose self-respect, surrender their virtue, cheapen themselves, and risk getting into trouble that will destroy their lives.

Let's recognize the sexual orientation of today's world for what it is. Like those before us who believed in a flat world concept or slavery, like those in other cultures who have bound their feet or put plates in their lips to stretch them, sexual promiscuity is the mistaken cultural practice of an unenlightened world. It is evil because it blunders across eternal laws and is doomed to make its practitioners miserable.

The challenge for young people and their families is to learn to withstand the pressures and influences that would degrade them. Young people have to find the courage to say no. A young woman wrote the following letter to her date after she had stuck to her standards:

"Dear Jim,

"Last night you pleaded with me, so ardently and urgently, to 'prove my love for you.' You were very persuasive, and because I always want to please you and do what you want me to do, it was hard to deny you.

"Today I am thankful from the bottom of a frightened and full heart that I did not let you persuade me. If I had agreed to your insistence, I would now be despising myself and hating and blaming you.

"I have hardly slept during the night, but I have thought

a lot. I kept thinking what a shining and beautiful word the word *purity* is. Today I do not believe that I could bear the despair and self-disgust that I would have felt if I had given in to you.

"All night, passages of scripture kept going through my mind, and they have never been so meaningful! The one that I thought of first was the one in which our Heavenly Father says, 'I, the Lord, delight in the chastity of women.' Today I can think of that scripture with deep thankfulness that it still applies to me! . . .

"I wonder if I could make you understand, a little, what you were asking. You are so very proud of your new sports car. What would you say if someone asked you to give her your car to prove your affection for her? You would surely think she was joking. Then if you found out that the person was in deadly earnest, you would know that she must be insane, yet you could get another car, and might be able to do so in less than a year. But if I had given you the gift of my chastity, I would have regretted it the rest of my life. You would have lost your purity, too. . . .

"Jim, I know that I will always think a lot of you, but now I feel that I cannot safely trust in you. Last night you were trying to destroy my purity and self-respect and chance of true future happiness, for a few minutes of excitement and pleasure for yourself. Your talk of my proving my love for you was a bitter mockery. You proved that you do not love me. You love only yourself." The letter is signed "Elizabeth." (*Improvement Era*, September 1970, p. 51.)

In a world where everything seems to change, may we have the courage to follow God's unchanging laws.

Index